B.I.G

Boundless Empowered
Bodacious Intuitive Grandiose

Felice Hightower Britt

Copyright © 2024

All Rights Reserved

ISBN: 979-8-89212-817-9

Dedication

This book is dedicated to my mother, the most loving, giving, and selfless person I know. I want her to know she has always been loved, not just by Christ but by me as well. Love you, Mommie.

Acknowledgment

To my first love, Jesus Christ, who planted the Be BIG seed in my spirit and has guided me thus far and will be with me and guide me all the way. I want to acknowledge my husband, Nelson Britt, who met me on the dance floor. I thank you for who you are. For you are a true gentleman, and thank you for providing the space for me to blossom not only in my BIG but to do and make BIG happen. To my mother, Phyllis, who is the epitome of love and resilience. No matter how hard and unkind life has been to you, you never stopped moving forward because of your deep love for your children, family, and others. I pray I make you proud as I am a product of your love and wonder. I thank God for the gift and legacy of my beautiful daughter, Najah. Your love motivates me to do BIG things so you will know what is possible.

To my granddaughter and clone, Anah, thank you for the love I knew was possible, your willingness to assist me without hesitation, and for being my foodie partner. Thank you to my brothers, James and Peter. You were the two main loving and consistent men in my life. You are an example of what men should be, and I never doubted your love and still don't. You are my heart, and I love you both. To Belinda, the sister I desired in my youth, thank you for loving me and accepting me fully, just as I am, and thank you for returning the favor of supporting me in this Be BIG journey. To my Sister Sonya, thank you for loving me through some of the most difficult times in my life and for modeling that things always work out.

I must acknowledge my strategist, Shennice Cleckley, who started the Be BIG book ball rolling and helped me get it done. This book would not have been accomplished without your accountability and direction. To my dad, who was there as much as he could be and gave me my love for books. Books have helped to shape me and build upon my gifts to my many mentors who have deposited seeds of wisdom, support, encouragement, and direction. I am forever grateful because your example is a part of my Be BIG. I would be here all day if I named all of you because many of you don't even know I considered you as mentors, but your deposits never went unnoticed, and I applied everything you deposited to me.

To my clients who crystallized my gifts and allowed me to be a part of your short-term or long-term journeys, I count all of it a privilege. Thank you for your grace and understanding that, despite being a therapist, I am first a human. To everyone who reads this book, my prayer is that you, too, develop a desire to discover and walk in your BIG. To all the people who have contributed to shaping me into BIG, I thank you. The good, bad, ugly, and indifferent, I wouldn't change a thing as it is why I am here. Today.

Last but not least, thank you to my grandmother, Nonnie. You love me so much. Even from above, I see you in my dreams and unexpected places, encouraging me to stay with God. I am forever your pudding cake, applesauce, and candy.

About the Author

Felice Hightower Britt is a Licensed Clinical Mental Health Counselor, Certified Clinical Trauma Professional, and certified life coach specializing in assisting individuals, couples, and families in resolving issues that hinder fulfilling and enduring relationships and prevent the realization of the life they desire and deserve.

With over fifteen years of experience, Felice has supported clients dealing with communication problems, financial issues, trust concerns, parenting differences, adolescent behavior issues, and trauma.

She is the founder of Resiliency Therapeutic Services, a private practice; Be BIG Coach, a coaching practice; and Real Talk With Felice. Felice conducts focus groups tailored to young ladies and women and has established the Be BIG Collective Community. Additionally, she hosted her talk show, Real Talk With Felice, and is a regular contributor to WBTV and various other news outlets such as WCNC, WFAE, and Scripps News.

Felice serves as an Executive Trainer for nonprofit and for-profit businesses/organizations, a motivational speaker, an advocate for Autism and individuals challenged with IDD, and an author.

Furthermore, Felice is passionate about classic films, and a noteworthy fun fact is her experience as a guest host programmer on Turner Classic Movies. She had the unique opportunity to interview former host Robert Osborne at the 2012 TCM Classic Film Festival. Felice is also the founder of the YANA Healing Circle and YANA Movement, the Be BIG Collective, and co-founder of the non-profit State(s) of Wellness Inc.

Contents

Dedication i
Acknowledgment ii
About the Author v
Chapter 1: My BIG Hindrance 1
Chapter 2: Forgiveness 14
Chapter 3: Invisible 23
Chapter 4: Colorism 32
Chapter 5: Life Just Ain't Fair 42
Chapter 6: Finding My Voice 58
Chapter 7: What Do You See? 68
Chapter 8: Big As External Perception 77
Chapter 9: BIG as an Internal Perception 84
Chapter 10: Defining BIG 97
Chapter 11: How To Be Big? 110
Chapter 12: See Yourself The Way God Sees You. 123
Chapter 13: Decide to see yourself BIG! 136
Chapter 14: Create A Like-Minded Village 148
Chapter 15: Determine To Stretch Yourself 167
Chapter 16: Examples of When to Be Big 174
Chapter 17: Who Is Big? 182
Chapter 18: What's Your BIG? 192
Chapter 19: Conclusion 211

Chapter 1: My BIG Hindrance

Imagine a world where everyone is living their lives to the fullest. Everyone is bold, courageous, and true to themselves. Everyone uses their gifts and talents to leave a positive imprint on the world. This is the vision God has for us. He fashioned us for greatness and intended for us to lead lives brimming with purpose and passion.

So, why not live your life to the fullest then?

Why not be Big in all ways?

And what does it mean to 'Be Big'?

"Being BIG" means living your life to its utmost potential, staying true to your authentic self, and employing your gifts and talents to leave a lasting impact on the world. It's about not letting fear or self-doubt deter you. It signifies being audacious and fearless in your pursuits.

So, why not Be Big?

You might chuckle at my rhetorical question, but I'm genuinely serious. In my life, I've seen countless individuals conjure reasons to diminish their shine instead of embracing the grandeur and boldness with which God intended us all to live. There are many reasons why people might choose to dim their light and not live their lives to the fullest. Some people are afraid of failure. Others are afraid of what other people will think. Still, others simply don't believe in themselves. But there are many more reasons why you should be big. You are more likely to achieve your goals and dreams when you are big. You are also more likely to inspire others to do the same. And when you are living your life to the fullest, you are more likely to be happy and fulfilled.

I'm a proud child of God, and I'm not ashamed to say it. But you don't have to be a Christian to get something out of this book. If you can just open your mind and heart to the messages and themes shared throughout this book, you will find wisdom and strength laced throughout the pages. Hopefully, you will experience a stirring inside your soul and a burning desire to want more for yourself in every dimension of your being.

I believe we are all connected and have a role to play in the grand scheme. We are all part of something bigger than ourselves.

I believe this book can change your life if you're open to it. This book is about helping you to understand your place in the universe and to live your life to the fullest. It's about helping you to be the best version of yourself and to make a difference in the world. I am a child of God and believe I am called to be big. I am called to dream big, live big, love big, encourage big, teach big, give big, and think big. But I didn't always feel this way. It took me a long time to realize my full potential. But when I finally did, I decided to embrace it. I was born into this world via the vehicle called trauma. I was a domestic violence baby and came into the world early due to the trauma my mother endured when she was pregnant with me. But I didn't let my traumatic beginnings define me. I chose to use my trauma as fuel and be BIG instead.

I decided to live my life as authentic, transparent, and real as possible. I chose to be BIG, live my life to the fullest, and make a difference in the world. I hope this book is a part of the change I desire to see in my community and world.

I believe I received my epiphany when I was supposed to, not a day later or a day before. I believe that God has perfectly orchestrated my journey and I am grateful for my experiences, both good and bad, as they have made me the person I am today, and I am excited to see what the future holds.

Trudging down memory lane when I look back over my life, sometimes the memories of my dad flash before me. I can remember my father being a pretty violent man. He would beat my mother over the most minor things.

One day, when my mother was pregnant with me, she saw a worm on a can of corn. She screamed, but instead of helping her, my father attacked her. As a result, my mother went into premature labor and gave birth to me earlier than expected. The nurses called me a warrior because I didn't require an incubator. I'm convinced that God had His hand on me from the very start.

What the devil meant for evil; God turned around for my good. My father's limitations became my power, and I beat the odds to not only survive the trauma but also to thrive. Unfortunately, the traumatic childbirth wasn't enough for my mother to leave my father. She stayed with him for many years, and I also endured his violence.

How do you forgive this type of witnessed trauma? People's inability to forgive stems from their "feelings" being in charge of them, but forgiveness is an act of one's personal will.

I want to express that my parents weren't terrible; they were simply human beings with their own flaws. My inability to forgive my mother stemmed from my belief that she should have left my father much earlier. In truth, my mom was aware that marrying my dad was a mistake, but she went against her gut feeling and altered the course of her life. I saw her postpone her dreams and struggle financially to provide for us and others, all because of that decision.

As for my father, my unforgiveness originated from his lack of emotional control and refusal to seek help. Despite being a self-educated man and an enthusiastic reader, he remained oblivious to the importance of getting assistance. Even though he could be seen as violent, I always felt secure around him. He was a masculine figure, physically fit and intimidating; no one dared to challenge him. Although he didn't possess a college degree, he could hold his own in conversations with highly educated individuals.

I share this because it's crucial to recognize that my father was not entirely evil, and I did grow up learning about various aspects of him. His example acted as a template for my future relationships – admittedly not too many but sufficient – which drew me towards eloquent yet emotionally distant tough guys. These were men with whom true love would remain elusive.

So, forgiveness became the key to unlocking my freedom and allowing myself to accept the goodness I know I deserve. My love for both of my parents runs deep despite our complex relationship that only a higher power can truly comprehend.

But I survived. And I thrived. I am a fighter. And I am a survivor.

Growing up, I witnessed the harrowing abuse my mother tolerated at my father's hands. These traumatic experiences left a permanent mark on my naive mind. I distinctly remember vowing never to follow in my mother's footsteps of tolerating violence from a man. It was utterly incomprehensible to me how someone who professed love could inflict such pain to the point where the other person could stand on the verge of dying.

The constant atmosphere of fear and uncertainty in our household was strangling. I recall one haunting night when my father's anger erupted to terrifying levels, culminating in him rendering my mother unconscious with the butt of his gun. I struggled to pinpoint my exact age during that dreadful moment, but I know I was younger than eight because my father left us alone when I was around that age.

The sheer terror and helplessness courting through my young veins during such incidents were overwhelming. My frantic, childlike attempts to discern how I could protect my mother to ensure her safety are still etched in my memory. It was a time when I was forced to grapple with emotions and circumstances no child should ever have to endure.

In the innocence of my young mind, I instinctively turned to the faith I had seen practiced in the Church. Clutching the blessed oil I had witnessed the women use during their solemn rituals, I approached my unconscious mother with a heart full of desperation. With trembling hands, I gently rubbed the sacred oil over where my mother had been struck, offering sincere prayers.

I stood vigilantly by her side, my young heart pouring its petitions to God. It was a moment of profound faith and determination, a child's unwavering belief in the divine. As I continued to pray, my mother stirred, her eyelids fluttering open.

In that miraculous instant, it dawned on me that my prayers had been answered. I had been granted a tangible, life-saving miracle, and then I realized the incredible power of prayer. In my innocent eyes, it was clear that Jesus had intervened to keep my mother alive, reaffirming my faith in the face of unimaginable adversity.

As my faith began to take root and grow, another, darker emotion simultaneously took hold within me: unforgiveness. It was like a seed that found fertile ground in my spirit, directed towards both of my parents. This unforgiveness, I realized later, became a significant obstacle in my journey to embrace my full potential and purpose in life. I clung to it as if it were a badge of honor, a justification for the barriers I encountered on my path.

This grudge I harbored became a formidable hindrance influencing various aspects of my life. It played a central role in my struggles, preventing me from truly living up to my potential. It was the catalyst behind my ill-fated choices in romantic partners, the source of my battles with self-esteem and self-worth, and a driving force behind my financial struggles as a single parent. Moreover, this unforgiveness cast a shadow over my aspirations, dreams, and desires, impeding their realization in ways that left me perplexed and disheartened.

What does it mean to be big to you?

Amidst the chaos of this world, being big isn't just a personal goal; it's the essence of our characters' odysseys. It beckons us to reach for the stars, dream beyond the confines of our mundane lives, and ignite the transformative gleams that alter destinies.

The phrase "be big" holds multifaceted meanings. It may signify physical stature, power, or success, yet this phrase transcends, urging us to be audacious, to envision grandly, and to chase our dreams relentlessly. It implores us to be the best versions of ourselves, making an indelible mark on the world.

The significance of Being Big extends beyond personal aspirations.

This book is about becoming your grandest self and documenting my journey anyone can relate to. So, you do not need to share my faith, Christianity, to grasp my book's narrative.

This is my story of figuring out how to do what makes me come alive and share my unique value with the world. This book is a voyage into the exhilarating realms of self-discovery and personal growth. Thus, I invite you into my narrative, where I uncover the secret to living a life that truly resonates with my essence. My book isn't merely a chronicle of personal growth; it's an inspiring tale that urges you to dream grandly, to strive for the extraordinary, and to believe in your endless potential.

> *"There is inside you all of the potential to be whatever you want to be, all of the energy to do whatever you want to do."*
>
> *–Donna Levine*

The book delves into timeless themes—identity, purpose, and surmounting trauma—while offering practical advice on goal setting, forging relationships, and crafting a fulfilling existence.

Forgiveness: Cure to Deep Injuries

For me, this writing journey meant confronting a formidable adversary that had shadowed my life—unforgiveness. It had held me captive for too long, a burden that weighed me down and poisoned my thoughts and emotions. I knew it had to be addressed from the outset.

Unforgiveness had been my ever-present companion, an anchor halting my progress and a relentless shadow that loomed over my life. It festered, a poison within me. It was time to expose it for my healing and the readers who might find solace in my words.

In these early pages, I share how unforgiveness scarred me, sowing pain and resentment in my heart. It's a vulnerability I embrace and raw honesty meant to resonate with those wrestling with similar demons.

Forgiveness, the seemingly simple act of letting go, has been my most formidable adversary, an invisible barrier that, for years, held me captive. It's a struggle that's deeply personal and profoundly human.

I carried the weight of grudges and resentments like a burden strapped to my back. Each injustice, every hurtful word, and the pain inflicted upon me festered within my heart, poisoning my thoughts and emotions.

This burden was especially heavy because it was born from deeply personal wounds. I had been wronged, betrayed, and hurt in ways that left scars both seen and unseen. The scars on my heart were the most enduring, for they were etched with bitterness and anger.

It wasn't just about forgiving others; it was about forgiving myself, too. I blamed myself for not being strong enough, allowing others to hurt me, and carrying these wounds like a badge of shame. But then, as I continued the path of self-discovery and growth, I realized that forgiveness wasn't a sign of weakness; it was an act of immense strength. It was a choice to release the grip of the past, to unshackle myself from the chains of resentment, and to free my spirit from the prison of anger.

At first, I feared confronting forgiveness. I feared letting go of my grievances would mean letting those who had hurt me off the hook. I feared that forgiving myself would mean absolving myself of responsibility. But soon, I realized I could not move forward in my life if I let the baggage from my past hold me back.

"Darkness cannot drive out darkness; only light can do that. Hate cannot drive out hate; only love can do that."

-Martin Luther King, Jr.

On this transformative journey, I began to see forgiveness in a different light. It wasn't about excusing the wrongs or forgetting the pain. It was about acknowledging the past, understanding that people, including myself, are imperfect, and choosing to release the hold those past hurts had on me.

Forgiveness was not a one-time event but a process, a journey within itself. It required me to confront the pain, to feel it deeply, and then to release it. It demanded empathy for others, recognizing that hurt people hurt people and that we all carry our own burdens.

As I allowed forgiveness to take root within me, I noticed a profound shift. The weight that had burdened me for so long began to lift. The anger that had consumed me gradually gave way to a sense of peace. I felt lighter, like a heavy backpack had been taken off my shoulders.

Forgiveness wasn't about condoning the wrongs of the past; it was about choosing to move forward, reclaiming my power, and living a life free from the shackles of resentment. It was about granting myself the freedom to heal and to grow.

I realized that forgiveness wasn't a gift to those who had wronged me but to myself. It allowed me to break free from the cycle of pain and embrace the present moment with open arms.

I slowly realized that forgiveness wasn't about erasing the past but rewriting my future. It was about reclaiming my inner peace, happiness, and power. It was about choosing love over anger, compassion over bitterness, and growth over stagnation.

So, my biggest hindrance, unforgiveness, became my most profound lesson. It taught me that letting go is not a sign of weakness but courage. It showed me that forgiveness is not about forgetting; it's about choosing to heal and move forward. And in that choice, I found the freedom to become the best version of myself, unburdened by the weight of the past. As I delve deeper into my journey of forgiveness in the preceding chapters, I aim to narrate personal growth and attest to the transformative power of letting go. I want you to understand that, like me, you can confront your hindrances, embark on a healing path, and liberate yourself.

As I unearthed this profound wisdom, it became evident that its understanding transcended religious boundaries. Each insight seemed a mirror reflecting our shared human journey, irrespective of individual beliefs. The stories and lessons echo the struggles, aspirations, and triumphs that unite us all.

> *"It's one of the greatest gifts you can give yourself to forgive. Forgive everybody."*
>
> *–Maya Angelou*

Chapter 2: Forgiveness

You can't spend so much time and effort hating someone else. Therefore, when you forgive them, it is about YOU, not about them. A cord between the two of you will need to be broken when you decide to forgive that individual(s). You can love and pray for them, but be cautious about inviting them back into your life to avoid repeating the same error.

What does the Bible say about forgiveness?

Colossians 3:13 it says,

> *"Bear with each other and forgive whatever grievances you may have against one another. Forgive as the Lord forgave you."*

Most of us find it difficult to forgive others. When we are hurt, our instinct is to retreat in order to defend ourselves. We don't typically brim with mercy, grace, and understanding when we've been wronged.

Is it possible to choose to forgive?

Is it a mental or physical action?

Is it an emotion?

Is it a mental or emotional state?

You might be asking yourself a few of these questions right now.

However, you must keep in mind that certain people are not worth jeopardizing your blessings for. Remember that you are in charge of your blessings and that they will be delayed if it takes you years to forgive your neighbor for what they did to you more than five years ago just because you find it difficult to forgive.

I had to learn this lesson as well. Every day, I continue to learn. I am learning to break out from the stage of anger and hatred every time I wake up, leave for work, and return home.

What harm can holding grudges truly cause you?

Does it improve your life in any way, or does it just make you angrier?

To forgive takes a lot of FAITH, but once you develop that FAITH, you can sit back and watch as God blesses you. People who have their doubts won't try to discredit you since blessings keep coming.

I understood that this lingering unforgiveness was not a badge of honor. But a heavy burden that I needed to release to experience the life I knew I was destined for. It was a realization that would ultimately pave the way for personal growth and transformation.

As I delved deeper into my soul, a profound realization emerged – I knew better than to let unforgiveness control my life. Through my connection with God and a period of self-reflection, it became undeniably clear that I needed to forgive my parents consciously. I recognized that my unforgiving stance was a significant obstacle in my growth journey.

During this thoughtful journey, I gained a new perspective on my parents. I began to understand that they were shaped by their own life experiences and endured their share of trauma. It dawned on me that people can only do better when they know better, and those who have been hurt often unintentionally inflict pain on others. It's a vicious cycle.

This realization marked a turning point in my life. It wasn't about justifying their actions but acknowledging the human complexities that had shaped them. By choosing forgiveness, I freed myself from the burden of unforgiveness and allowed space for empathy and healing. It was a powerful act of liberation that set me on a path toward greater understanding and personal growth.

Even though I had this profound revelation about forgiveness, the decision to forgive wasn't any easier. I found myself grappling with the challenge even after I had committed to forgiveness. However, a crucial shift occurred when I realized that forgiveness is an immense strength, a manifestation of one's inner power.

I came to understand that forgiveness is a choice that empowers you to regain control of your life. It's a conscious decision to break free from the chains of your past to no longer be accountable for the actions of your abuser, rapist, molester, or perpetrator. It's not about granting them the satisfaction of seeing the error of their ways; instead, it's about declaring that you refuse to be a victim and they no longer have power over you now and over your future.

In essence, forgiveness becomes an instrument of liberation. It allows you to step out of the shadows of your past and embrace the fullness of your present. It's a declaration of independence from the haunting ghosts of your history, a commitment to move forward unburdened and unrestrained.

I'm here to share this message because I firmly believe that we deserve to live a life that's nothing short of magnificent and BIG in every sense. We were not meant to be held back or diminished by the scars of our past. Instead, we can choose to Be BIG and seize all the opportunities and joys life offers. We are meant to have and share in an experience that will follow us into eternity. It means our lives are not limited to this physical world or this lifetime. We are spiritual beings on a human journey, and our purpose is to grow and evolve our consciousness.

I don't believe I, a Spirit-filled woman with a human experience, was supposed to live this life small. As mentioned at the start of this chapter, we are all here to live our lives to the fullest, express our unique gifts and talents, and make a difference in the world. How can I call God, the great I AM, my Father, and live this life minuscule? Is that the way a child is to honor their Father? I don't think so. To praise our Father, God, we must live our lives to the fullest and reach our highest potential.

Well, not anymore, and quite frankly, playing limited is exhaustive and takes way more energy than expected, so why not do BIG? Playing small is draining because it is not our true nature. *We are meant to live significant lives, dream big dreams, and take substantial actions.*

So,

What does it mean to you to live a big life?

What are your dreams and aspirations?

What are you passionate about?

What are you good at?

How can you use your gifts and talents to make a difference in the world?

Start by taking some time to reflect on these questions. Once you understand what you want to achieve in life, you can create a plan to make it happen.

I've always been drawn to people who are comfortable in their skin. They don't try to be someone they're not. They embrace their quirks and imperfections. They're confident in their abilities and not afraid to take risks. These are the people who make the world a more exciting and vibrant place. They're the ones who stand out from the crowd and inspire others to be themselves.

For many years, I was afraid of many trivial things, such as,

Do I really have what it takes?

I've always been a dreamer with big goals and aspirations, with a desire to make a difference and leave a mark in the world.

Will I be successful?

Who am I to think of myself in that way?

What will people really think of me, and what could be BIG about me?

I'm not always the most confident person, but seeing someone living their life unapologetically gives me the courage to do the same. It reminds me that it's okay to be different. It's okay to be myself.

Yet, for a long time, I let my fears hold me back. I was afraid of failure. I feared rejection. I stressed about what other people would think of me if I failed. I doubted myself, and I questioned my abilities. I didn't think I was smart enough or talented enough to achieve my goals.

I don't remember exactly when I got tired of playing small and seeing myself as small. It was a gradual process, influenced by personal development and the mentorship of some amazing women.

I realized I had been playing small for so many years, doing just enough to get by and be accepted by others. But most importantly, I had accepted my own lies about my capabilities. In my own way, I was holding myself back from achieving my full potential.

I lived in two parallel worlds: one where I believed I was confident, self-assured, magnetic, gregarious, and well-rounded, and another where I was insecure, doubtful, polarizing, isolative, and limited.

I was optimistic, positive, and full of faith in my ideal world. In the real world, I was pessimistic, negative, and doubtful. If I had truly believed I was the woman in my ideal world, I would have chosen to be big, live big, and show up big many years ago.

Knowing I am not alone drives me to live my life fully. As a licensed counselor, I have heard countless stories from other women who have had similar experiences. This collective of women has inspired me to take my rightful place as the Be Big Coach. I am here to answer all of your questions about being BIG, including the why, how, when, and where of BIG. Being BIG is a word, a way of life, and a movement! I am proud to be a part of this collective of women empowering each other to live big lives. The word "BIG" means something different to different people. To me, being BIG is about living a life that is true to yourself, your values, and your dreams. It is about being courageous enough to step outside your comfort zone and go after what you want. It encapsulates authenticity, vulnerability, and the willingness to share your unique gifts with the world.

Embracing such a BIG life is no small feat. It demands courage, perseverance, and unwavering faith in oneself. Yet, the rewards are immeasurable. Living a BIG life not only brings personal happiness, fulfillment, and success but also creates ripples of positive change in the world.

I am a child of God and believe I am called to be big. I am called to dream big, live big, love big, encourage big, teach big, give big, and think big. I didn't always think this way. In fact, it took me a long time to realize my full potential. But when I finally did, I decided to embrace it.

I was born into a difficult situation. I was a domestic violence baby, and I came into the world early due to the trauma my mother experienced. But I didn't let my circumstances define me. I chose to be big. I chose to live my life to the fullest. And I chose to make a difference in the world.

I believe I received my epiphany when I was supposed to, not a day later. I believe that God has perfectly orchestrated my journey. I am grateful for my experiences, both good and bad. They have made me the person I am today. And I am excited to see what the future holds.

My father is a product of his past and its trauma, which contributed to his doing violent things, such as causing my mother to go into premature labor. I had been granted a tangible, life-saving miracle, and it was then that I realized the incredible power of prayer. In my young eyes, it was clear that Jesus had intervened to keep my mother alive, again, reaffirming my faith in the face of unimaginable adversity.

God said to do it in the following manner: Forgive us of OUR own sins as we also forgive others who have wronged us.

Therefore, when God gives you another chance to live, let forgiveness permeate every aspect of your day. Eventually, things will start to improve.

Chapter 3: Invisible

From my earliest memories, there was something unique about my perception of the world – I genuinely believed I was invisible. It was an odd notion that clung to me as I grew up in the Linden Houses projects, tucked away in the East New York section of Brooklyn. While some folks might label it as "the hood," for me, it was nothing less than home.

I remained blissfully unaware of the neighborhood's reputation until I was "bussed out" and saw firsthand how my white friends lived.

Oh, what a stark contrast it was.

Let me paint you a picture of Linden Houses: nineteen buildings sprawled over a vast thirty acres of land, composed of towering structures fashioned from brick, stone, and steel. The building I called home stood firm at eight floors, each housing eight units, and four were divided by robust, steel-screened balconies.

Residing in the Linden Houses, we had a single elevator to serve the entire building. It served as a lifeline for the 64 families who relied on it daily, but it was more than just a means of transport; it often turned into a communal chat room. Additionally, we had two staircases that helped keep us all reasonably fit.

Then there was the enigmatic "incinerator," a peculiar feature where we disposed of our trash. It was like a relic from another time, hidden inside a wall, complete with a fire-breathing dragon of a machine that devoured our refuse.

Our apartment was a cozy haven, complete with three bedrooms, a single bathroom, a comfortable living room, and a kitchen. A narrow hallway wove everything together, creating a sense of unity within those walls. My family's dwelling was on the third floor, facing the front of the building, and it afforded us a decent view of what we affectionately called "the circle." Within these walls and the vibrant community of the Linden Houses, I forged my childhood memories and learned the true meaning of home.

New York City, with its towering skyscrapers and bustling streets, is often referred to as the concrete jungle. It is a moniker that paints a picture of a place devoid of nature's touch, dominated by man-made steel, glass, and concrete structures. Yet, my memories of New York are far from this stark image.

Indeed, this city is an urban behemoth, a testament to human ambition and innovation. But in my recollections, this metropolis has a greener, softer side. I remember trees. Not just small city trees confined to sidewalks but big, sprawling ones. Their majestic branches spread wide, creating an urban canopy that coexisted harmoniously with the city's towering architecture. These trees were the silent watchers of the city's frantic pace, standing tall amid the hustle and bustle. They provided much-needed shade during the day, their leafy arms acting as a natural parasol against the harsh summer sun. But their role didn't end there. As the city transformed under the cloak of night, these trees took on a new purpose.

Hot summer nights in New York are a saga of their own. Having absorbed the day's heat, the city's concrete and steel structures radiate it back into the night, creating an urban heat island effect. But under the trees, it was a different story. Their dense foliage acted as a natural insulator, trapping cooler air beneath. A welcome draft flowed under these tree canopies, offering a respite from the sweltering city heat.

Conversely, during the cold months, our trusty radiators came into play. They were scattered throughout our unit, providing us with the coziest warmth during the chilly winter. These elements, the trees, and the radiators were like natural and man-made companions that painted the backdrop of my upbringing amid Brooklyn's bustling life.

"The circle" held a special place in my heart. It was the hub of my childhood, where I'd gather with my friends to engage in the fine art of discussing absolutely nothing, to crack jokes and tease each other relentlessly. It was a playground for our youthful spirits, a canvas for our favorite games like tag, punchbowl, punchanella, and double Dutch. The circle wasn't just a space but an adventure waiting to happen. With its monkey bars and barrels, it encouraged us to stay active, and on those scorching summer days, a sprinkler would rise like a guardian angel, granting us the sweet relief of cool water against the heat index. Those moments of shared laughter, friendly competition, and playful escapades are etched into my memory.

But the heart of it all was the sense of community in my hood. It wasn't just a place to live but a true home. Everyone in our neighborhood looked out for one another, creating a bond that transcended bricks and concrete. In the Linden Houses, I discovered a tight-knit family, and "the circle" was that extended family's living, breathing heart.

Those were different times back then. In our neighborhood, all parents had a collective right to set us straight, and disputes were settled through words and fists, not the menacing presence of guns. Our harsh winters sometimes turned "the circle" into an impromptu ice-skating rink, where laughter and joy replaced the everyday games.

Benches were thoughtfully scattered around, creating ideal spots for us to congregate. There, we'd share music and indulge in our beloved bodega snacks, each moment fostering deeper bonds.

Yet, within those very circle gatherings, I learned to toughen up, my skin grew thicker with each teasing comment. I was an easy target, primarily due to my appearance. Names like "blackie," "darkie," "big lips," "ugly," and "bald-headed" became part of my daily existence. At that age, I couldn't grasp the true beauty and power of my melanated skin, but those experiences, as harsh as they were, ultimately contributed to the development of my resilience and that subtle edge in my character.

Each insult was a jab at my identity, an attempt to make me feel lesser for the color of my skin, the shape of my lips, and my natural features. These were the formative years of my life, yet instead of basking in the joy of childhood, I was wrestling with comments that sought to diminish my sense of self-worth.

At that tender age, understanding the depth of racial prejudice or the concept of colorism was beyond my grasp. I was too young, too innocent, to comprehend that the very traits I was being ridiculed for were, in fact, the marks of my heritage, the symbols of my lineage, the undeniable signs of my ancestry. The melanin in my skin, the features of my lips, and the texture of my hair were not flaws or reasons for mockery. They were, and are, the embodiment of a rich history, a testament to the resilience and beauty of my people.

None of those hurtful labels were true, but as a young girl growing up in a single-parent household, with only my mother and grandmother to affirm my beauty, it was hard not to internalize those lies. "Sticks and stones may break my bones, but words will never hurt me" was a saying I'd heard, but the reality was quite different. Words do hurt, and they can cut deeper than any physical pain.

I recall shedding countless tears, my heart aching as their words sliced through my spirit. Being a deeply melanated girl, I was repeatedly described as "blackie" or "darkie." It felt like an unrelenting assault on my self-esteem, as if the world conspired to make me question my worth. Despite the love and reassurance from my mother and grandmother, the harsh judgments from others often overshadowed their words of comfort. It was a poignant lesson in how words, even when untrue, can wield a remarkable power to wound and shape our self-perception.

Today, those hurtful words hold no power over me, but the world seemed different back then. While not the pervasive force it is today, television played a significant role in shaping my perceptions. However, the programming in those days had limited diversity, and it would usually sign off at around midnight. What little was on TV often lacked representation of individuals who looked like me. Images of white people with blonde hair and blue eyes dominated the screens. This lack of representation had a profound impact on me and many other melanated girls. We weren't treated the same, and there was a prevailing bias in favor of white or light-skinned black girls. They seemed to receive more attention and admiration and were regarded as the standard of beauty within the Black community. It was as though the deeper shades of melanin were overlooked, leaving girls like me feeling invisible, not just to the world but even within our own community. Those early experiences sowed seeds of self-doubt that took years to uproot.

Those messages I heard in my childhood left a lasting imprint on me, shaping my mindset and behavior. I found myself trying to stay beneath the radar, hoping that by shrinking a bit, I could evade the hurtful names and judgments. It was a strategy of self-preservation, a defense mechanism to avoid another day of growing up. I witnessed a stark disparity in how girls of different skin tones were treated. There was a hierarchy, a color scale, with white and light-skinned black girls at the top, receiving the lion's share of attention and admiration. In the Black community, they were often held up as the standard of beauty, their features and skin tones glorified. On the other hand, we melanated girls were relegated to the sidelines. Our beauty was overlooked, our worth underestimated, and our voices quieted. This bias wasn't just societal but deeply ingrained within our community. It was in the childhood messages we often heard, the subtle hints, and the overt statements that slowly but surely chipped away at our self-esteem. These messages, whether intentional or not, promoted a singular, narrow definition of beauty – a definition that didn't include girls like me with our rich, melanated skin.

In response to these biases, I tried to stay under the radar to make myself smaller and less noticeable. The logic was simple: if I drew less attention to myself, I could escape the painful experience of being called an ugly name. It was a defense mechanism, a cloak of invisibility I donned to protect myself from the sting of prejudice and colorism.

Despite the strides we've made over the years in terms of representation and inclusivity, it's disheartening to see that too much still hasn't changed. The echoes of those childhood messages persist, reverberating in the representation we see in media and popular culture today. Melanated images - images of dark-skinned individuals- are still underrepresented, overshadowed by a dominance of white, light-skinned, or mulatto images.

It's like the past is repeating itself, and the cycle of marginalization continues. The spotlight still predominantly shines on white or light-skinned individuals, while melanated individuals are left in the shadows. This uneven representation perpetuates harmful stereotypes and upholds the skewed standards of beauty that have long haunted our community.

This is not to dismiss the progress we have made. There are more diverse representations now than there were decades ago, and we've seen the rise of influential melanated figures in the media, politics, and other fields. But it's clear that there's still a long way to go.

We need to continue challenging these biases and advocating for more balanced representation. We need to elevate melanated voices, images, and stories and broaden the definition of beauty to include the diversity of all skin tones. We need to ensure that no child has to shrink themselves to escape prejudice and that every individual feels seen, valued, and beautiful in their unique identity. Ending the pain of being labeled as "ugly."

Chapter 4: Colorism

Colorism in America is prevalent, meaning that it is widespread and common. It is a form of prejudice or discrimination against individuals with a darker skin tone, typically among people of the same ethnic or racial group. Colorism is often rooted in the belief that lighter skin is more attractive, desirable, and superior to darker skin. This belief is often perpetuated by Eurocentric beauty standards, which have been embedded in American culture for centuries.

Colorism manifests itself in many different ways in American society. For example, studies have shown that people with darker skin tones are more likely to be perceived as less intelligent, competent, and trustworthy. They are also more likely to be discriminated against in employment, housing, and education. Colorism can also lead to negative health outcomes, such as increased stress and depression.[1] Colorism is a deeply ingrained issue that extends beyond the United States and affects societies worldwide. The old children's rhyme reflects the

---

[1] https://phys.org/news/2020-03-skin-tone-scars-asian-americans.html

historical bias and discrimination associated with skin color.

> *"If you're black, stay back.*
>
> *If you're brown, stick around.*
>
> *If you're yellow, you're mellow.*
>
> *If you're white, you're all right."*

1. **"If you're black, stay back"**: This line conveys the unfortunate reality of how black individuals have often faced systemic discrimination, prejudice, and racial injustice. It has roots in the historical legacies of slavery, segregation, and ongoing racism.

2. **"If you're brown, stick around"**: This part suggests that individuals with brown skin may encounter less severe discrimination compared to black individuals. However, they still face biases and challenges, especially in regions with diverse populations.

3. **"If you're yellow, you're mellow"**: This phrase is used to describe people of Asian descent. While it might seem less discriminatory, it perpetuates stereotypes and objectification of Asian people, reducing their complex identities to a simplified caricature.

4. **"If you're white, you're all right"**: This line reinforces the privilege historically afforded to those with lighter skin. White individuals have often

experienced fewer obstacles and advantages in various aspects of life. Addressing colorism means acknowledging these stereotypes and biases and the impact they have on individuals and societies. Working toward a more inclusive and equitable world where skin color does not determine one's worth or opportunities is essential.

During slavery in the United States, individuals with lighter skin, commonly referred to as "mulattoes" or "house slaves," often received preferential treatment compared to those with darker skin. Several factors drove this preference:

1. **White-European Beauty Standards:** Slaveholders, who were predominantly of European descent, imposed European beauty standards on their enslaved population. Lighter skin was associated with European ancestry and was considered more attractive.

2. **Closer Resemblance to Slave Owners:** Lighter-skinned individuals were sometimes the offspring of liaisons between enslavers and enslaved women. They were more likely to resemble their white fathers, which sometimes led to preferential treatment.

3. **Indoor vs. Outdoor Work:** Lighter-skinned slaves were often assigned to work inside the plantation owner's house, performing domestic tasks. This provided them with slightly better living

conditions and reduced exposure to the harsh conditions of field labor that darker-skinned slaves endured.

4. Social Status: Lighter-skinned individuals were often given more education opportunities and sometimes had a higher social status within the enslaved community.

These distinctions based on skin color created a hierarchical system within the enslaved population, deepening divisions and perpetuating the notion that lighter skin was superior to darker skin. Over time, these biases evolved and persisted, becoming ingrained in various societies and cultures worldwide, not limited to the United States.

Today, colorism continues to manifest itself in many aspects of life, from beauty standards and media representation to job opportunities and social interactions. Efforts to combat colorism involve raising awareness, promoting inclusivity, and challenging these deeply ingrained prejudices.

The historical practice of favoring individuals with lighter skin over those with darker skin during slavery in the United States left a lasting impact on society. This preference was not only a reflection of deeply ingrained racial biases but also the imposition of European beauty standards on enslaved populations. Lighter skin, which was associated with

European ancestry, was deemed more attractive, and those with it were often considered more favorable. This created a hierarchy among enslaved individuals, with those of lighter skin sometimes receiving better treatment, education, and opportunities as they more closely resembled the white slave owners. These distinctions based on skin color have had long-lasting consequences, perpetuating the belief that lighter skin is superior to darker skin.

Today, the legacy of colorism is still visible in many aspects of contemporary society. In media, including TV, commercials, and social media, there is a persistent bias towards individuals with lighter skin tones. Beauty standards and media representation often favor lighter-skinned individuals, which can lead to the underrepresentation or misrepresentation of people with darker skin tones. This continued preference perpetuates the feeling of invisibility among those with darker skin, as they are less likely to see themselves reflected in the media and may internalize harmful stereotypes or feelings of inadequacy.

This unequal representation and ongoing bias in favor of lighter skin contribute to a complex web of societal challenges. It reinforces a harmful message that equates lightness with beauty and success while marginalizing those with darker skin tones. As a result, society needs to recognize and address this issue, promoting diversity and inclusivity to ensure that all skin tones are celebrated and valued. Efforts to challenge these deeply rooted prejudices involve increasing awareness of colorism, encouraging diverse representation in media, and celebrating individuals' beauty and worth regardless of skin color. Only by collectively addressing and dismantling these harmful biases can we strive for a more equitable and inclusive society.

I can relate to the feeling of becoming somewhat invisible to my peers, and, like you, I found myself unintentionally contributing to it as a way to avoid being singled out or picked on. As a means of self-preservation, it's not uncommon to withdraw or intentionally fade into the background in social situations, especially when faced with the fear of judgment or criticism.

This tendency to fly under the radar often stems from a desire to avoid the spotlight, which can sometimes come with the burden of unwanted attention or scrutiny. I remember moments when I would downplay my achievements or opinions, choosing to blend in rather than stand out. This self-imposed invisibility seemed like a shield against potential criticism or rejection, a way to protect myself from the vulnerability of being seen and judged.

Yet, as time went on, I realized that while this coping mechanism might have provided temporary relief from negative attention, it also limited my personal growth and hindered authentic connections with others. It's essential to strike a balance between self-preservation and self-expression. Being "invisible" to peers may protect us from potential harm. Still, it can also hinder opportunities for genuine connections, personal development, and the ability to stand up for what we believe in.

Over time, I began to recognize the importance of finding my authentic voice and expressing myself without fear. It's a process that involves embracing vulnerability and acknowledging that it's okay to be visible, seen as imperfect, and stand up for what I believe in. It's about gradually shedding the self-imposed invisibility cloak and stepping into the light, even if it feels daunting at times. It's a journey towards self-acceptance and the understanding that being true to oneself is more empowering and fulfilling than blending into the background to avoid potential judgment.

From a very early age, I found myself surrounded by a circle of friends who exuded confidence, beauty, and popularity, most of them having lighter or "red-boned" skin. It's intriguing to reflect on how this dynamic took shape because it has been all of my life since I started making friends. Nevertheless, it has been a recurring theme throughout my life, and it's profoundly impacted how I perceive myself and my sense of uniqueness.

I couldn't help but notice that being in the company of these friends made me feel special, too. It was as if their attributes somehow reflected positively on me. Their confidence was infectious, and their popularity seemed to rub off on me by association. There was an unspoken understanding that being part of this particular group had its own set of advantages, and it bolstered my self-esteem.

Yet, as time went on, I began to question this dynamic. I realized that my worth shouldn't be solely dependent on the company I keep or the appearance of my friends. It's important to remember that our individual worth is not defined by our social circles or skin color. Each of us has unique qualities, talents, and experiences that make us special in our own right.

As I grew older, I started focusing on developing my self-confidence, embracing my identity, and valuing myself independently of external influences. While friendships are important and can be empowering, it's crucial to recognize that our self-worth should come from within. I learned that I am special because of who I am, not just because of the people I choose to surround myself with. This realization has been a crucial step in my journey towards self-acceptance and a deeper understanding of my own unique value. It's not uncommon to feel like an observer in your own life, especially when you're surrounded by friends who attract attention and admiration from others. That was me on the sidelines, watching people as they were drawn to my friends while I remained in the background, feeling small and, quite frankly, "invisible."

This dynamic can be a double-edged sword. On the one hand, being accepted by your popular and confident friends is undoubtedly a form of validation, indicating that you, too, have qualities that make you an appealing person. It's a reminder that you are worthy of their friendship. However, on the other hand, it can sometimes overshadow your individuality and make you feel like you're constantly living in their shadow.

Feeling small or invisible can be challenging, as it may lead to a sense of self-doubt and an underestimation of your own worth. Recognizing that your uniqueness and value aren't contingent on the people you associate with or their popularity is essential. Your qualities, experiences, and contributions make you special in your own right.

Over time, as I've come to understand, it's important to strike a balance between appreciating the positive aspects of these friendships and asserting your own identity. You have the agency to step into the spotlight, express your thoughts and passions, and claim your place in the world. It's a journey towards recognizing that you are not small or invisible but rather an individual with your strengths, dreams, and the potential to influence the world uniquely. It's about finding the confidence to be seen for who you truly are beyond the influence of others.

My journey, thus far, has caused me to realize that I was never invisible. I was always seen by those who truly loved me, such as my Mother, siblings, grandmother, and closest friends. But, most importantly, I was always seen, loved, and accepted by God. So, I proclaim to the Universe and encourage you to do the same. I am not invisible by any means. I am seen, and I am loved. Deeply.

Chapter 5: Life Just Ain't Fair

Not having money further contributed to my perceived smallness as I was considered poor. Growing up, my mom didn't bring home a lot of money, which profoundly impacted my life. It meant I didn't have the luxury of having up-to-date clothes or the latest sneakers. To most kids, those might seem like minor things, but in my world, they were pivotal.

Having the right sneakers was more than just a fashion statement – it was a rite of passage. The schoolyard was a battlefield of brands and styles, where kids wore their sneakers like badges of honor. It was a culture of coolness that I desperately wanted to be a part of, but financial constraints pulled me further away from that elusive realm.

The lack of money amplified the differences between me and my peers, making me feel even more invisible. When your classmates sported the latest Adidas Superstars, Filas, Pumas, and Nike, and you had generic, non-descript sneakers, it was hard not to feel like you were from another world. Their footwear represented status, self-assuredness, and a sense of belonging. For me, it symbolized my exclusion, a constant reminder that I couldn't keep up.

I'd lie in bed many nights, staring at the ceiling, and ask God why. Why was I the one left out? Why did money have to be such a defining factor in my life, in my worth? I knew my mom was doing her best, working tirelessly to provide for our family, but it was tough seeing her struggle, and it was equally challenging trying to fit in with my peers.

However, these experiences also taught me valuable lessons about resilience, empathy, and the power of determination. They shaped me into someone who understands that material possessions don't determine true worth. The invisible, small kid has grown into someone who understands the depth of people's character and the importance of inner strength.

So, while I can't deny that my past had its share of hardships, those very trials made me who I am today – someone who values compassion, grit, and the ability to stand out in a world where fitting in was once an unattainable dream.

Why didn't He make me like white people, or at least light-skinned? Why would He put me in a skin color that is seen as ugly by the masses or less than? These questions haunted me for years, like an unrelenting shadow in the background of my life. I couldn't change my skin color, and it felt like an indelible mark I had no say in. Everywhere I turned, I was acutely aware of the way I was perceived negatively because of my skin. I can still vividly remember those nights when I cried myself to sleep, feeling utterly alone in my journey. Most of my early childhood friends were lighter skinned, some even white, and it seemed like they lived in an entirely different world. They were the ones who effortlessly garnered attention and were treated better by boys. Adults seemed to favor them, and they always seemed to have more money to spend on those nice, trendy clothes I could only dream of owning.

It wasn't just about the color of our skin; it was about the privilege that came with it. I couldn't help but feel like an outsider in a game I never signed up to play. It was as if the world had assigned a value to my worth based on something I had no control over. I yearned for the days when I could blend in when the content of my character mattered more than the shade of my skin.

Over time, I realized that the problem wasn't with me or my skin; it was with a society that often clings to shallow judgments and stereotypes. I learned that true beauty lies in diversity, that no skin color is better than another, and that worth should never be measured by the shade of your complexion.

My journey has been one of self-discovery, resilience, and a fierce determination to challenge the preconceived notions that society can impose. I've grown into someone who values the unique qualities that make me who I am, embracing the richness of my heritage and the stories woven into the tapestry of my skin.

I spent a significant part of my formative years indoors, where my sanctuary was the world of books. Reading was my escape from the harsh realities of the outside world, and I found solace in the pages of countless stories. As I immersed myself in these narratives, I noticed a transformation within myself that would ultimately shape my identity.

I wasn't blessed with what society deemed as "pretty" by conventional standards, but I quickly realized that being smart could be my thing. While my fair-skinned girlfriends were admired for their beauty, I discovered that my intelligence was a different kind of beauty, a power all its own. It was an advantage, a weapon I could wield in a world where my complexion was often seen as a limitation.

Being placed in gifted classes, I often found myself surrounded by predominantly white classmates, sometimes being the sole black student or one of just a few. In these settings, I became aware of the stark contrast between what I had to offer and what society expected from me. I embraced my role as a smart, driven student who was determined to excel. It was my way of saying, "I may not fit your narrow beauty standards, but I have something just as valuable to offer."

It wasn't about diminishing the intelligence of my fair-skinned friends; many of them were incredibly bright. However, I recognized that their fair complexions often became a double-edged sword. It was a distraction they couldn't control, and it divided their attention. While they juggled the expectations of beauty and brains, I had the freedom to hone in on my education without such distractions.

My focus on academics became my source of strength, my refuge. I knew knowledge was a passport to opportunities, and I intended to seize them with all my might. In those gifted classes, I was not just the smart kid; I was the one who broke stereotypes and defied expectations. I showed that brilliance could shine brightly in any shade.

Over time, I learned that beauty is diverse, encompassing more than just outward appearances. It's found in the depths of knowledge, the resilience of character, and the determination to defy society's constraints. My journey as the "smart one" fueled my intellectual growth and became a powerful reminder that my worth extended far beyond the confines of skin-deep judgments.

The memory of the day my dad left is etched in my mind like a scar. It was a moment that rocked the foundation of our family, leaving me feeling a whirlwind of emotions. I was just a child, and the world as I knew it was crumbling around me.

As my dad walked away, the weight of his absence pressed down on my heart. He had always been our protector, a New York City police officer with a reputation as a real badass. No one messed with Hightower, and his departure left an ominous void in our lives. The sense of security he provided seemed irreplaceable.

My dad wasn't just a formidable figure but an embodiment of strength and knowledge. He had a passion for martial arts, and his prowess in that field was matched only by his love for books. It's my dad I credit for my own deep-seated affection for literature. He was a voracious reader, and his ability to talk about virtually anything, thanks to his love of books, left a profound mark on me.

He was my hero, guiding light, and singular model of what a man should be. But he was gone, and I was left with a deluge of questions and uncertainties. Did he not love me anymore? What did I do to drive him away? What could I do to bring him back? These questions swirled in my young mind like a never-ending storm.

As I look back on that period, I realize that his departure wasn't a reflection of my worth but rather a complex tapestry of adult choices and circumstances. It took years to understand that sometimes, even our heroes are faced with battles they can't win, and they, too, need to find their path.

My dad's absence left a void, but it shaped me unexpectedly. It ignited my curiosity, love for books, and the quest to be a protector in my own right. Over time, I understood that his love for us didn't vanish with his physical presence. It remained a constant force in my life, guiding me through challenges and encouraging me to seek strength in knowledge and family bonds.

The separation of my parents was like a seismic shift in my world, one that I couldn't quite comprehend as a child. The absence of any explanation made it even more bewildering, leaving me to navigate the turbulent waters of my emotions on my own. I was left to piece together the puzzle of our family's unraveling, and the conclusions I arrived at were a mix of deep sorrow, anger, and resentment.

But I realized that bitterness was a path I didn't want to tread. Instead, I sought solace in a different kind of presence – that of Jesus. Faith became my sanctuary, a way to channel my emotions into something positive, a source of strength amid turmoil.

In the wake of my dad's departure, I became my mom's right-hand man. It was a role I didn't choose but one that circumstances thrust upon me. My siblings and I became her responsibility, and I, at a tender age, assumed the duties and responsibilities that traditionally and developmentally belonged to a parent. It was a process known as parentification, and it transformed me into a young caretaker, far beyond what I should have been at that age. As a latchkey kid, I learned to swallow fear like a bitter pill. My afternoons were no longer filled with carefree play. Instead, they were marred by a sense of decorum and responsibility, a larger-than-life personality, a fun nature, and intelligence that no child should bear. I had to become the dependable presence my siblings could rely on when our world seemed unstable.

However, I always felt restricted in my ability to express myself fully because people always reminded me how loud I could be. This parentification was born out of necessity, a response to the void left by my parents' separation. There was no one else to step in and help keep our family together, so I stepped up. It wasn't a path I chose, but it became a defining chapter in my life, shaping me into someone who understood the importance of resilience, sacrifice, and the unbreakable bonds of family.

My mother's love for me led her to make a decision that would significantly shape my childhood and adolescence. She was determined to ensure that I received an education equal to, or better than, my white peers, so she had me "bussed out" of our neighborhood to attend a predominantly white school. This choice had profound consequences, further deepening my sense of invisibility on multiple levels.

At this new school, the first level of invisibility was the lack of acceptance. It wasn't merely the cold shoulders of my peers but also the indifference from the adults, the administration, and the staff. It was as though I was an unwanted intruder in a world that didn't quite know how to embrace someone like me. While children tend to be naturally accepting, this environment had less receptive adults, which left me feeling like an outsider.

The second level was the challenge of navigating this foreign world that didn't seem to want me. I had to learn how to survive in a place that made it clear I didn't quite belong. It meant adapting to norms and expectations that often clashed with my own experiences.

The third level was the most intricate: how to assimilate back into my neighborhood without drawing attention or ridicule. It was a delicate balancing act, living in two worlds with different expectations and norms, where I was made to feel both invisible and conspicuously different simultaneously.

I use the term "purposeful invisibility" because it was evident that I was not meant to feel welcome or accepted. This perception wasn't solely due to my white peers, who were, after all, just children. Racism and hate are learned behaviors, often instilled by fearful adults' intent on preserving the status quo. I was rarely acknowledged or called upon, serving as an example of what not to be. Please grant me some grace as I share these memories, for they come from the perspective of a child between the ages of six and eleven. They may not be entirely accurate, but they capture my emotional reality. I entered an environment that, overall, didn't welcome me. This sense of not belonging was further accentuated by the fact that, aside from two remarkable exceptions, Mr. Shaw, my fifth-grade teacher who was black, and Mr. Pass, my music teacher who was white, the other teachers merely tolerated me and the other black students out of necessity.

I remember a particularly painful incident in third grade when my teacher, Mrs. Marks, slapped me in front of the class, wrongly believing that I had instigated an incident that caused laughter. It wasn't me, but my mother's intervention prompted her to apologize, a desperate attempt to rectify the harm and restore some sense of power. In retrospect, Mrs. Marks' actions were fueled by her privilege, ego, and, yes, what I can only describe as a form of hatred. It might seem harsh to label it as such, but what else could motivate a grown-up to strike an eight-year-old child for causing laughter in a classroom? Her actions spoke of dominance, contempt, and disrespect.

I firmly believe that had she known that the true instigator of that laughter was a white child, she would not have raised a hand. Her actions, whether fueled by pride, ego, or a deep-seated prejudice, were a stark reminder of the discrimination that could rear its head in even the most unexpected of places. During those formative years, this experience and many others taught me the importance of challenging prejudice, fostering understanding, and fighting against the silent injustices that can persist when left unaddressed.

The memory of that moment when Mrs. Marks slapped me in front of my white peers is something that never left me. It was a stark reminder of the vulnerability and isolation I often felt during those formative years. It was not just a physical act but a traumatic experience that cut deep into my sense of self-worth.

That slap disrupted my notion of invisibility, but not in a way anyone should ever experience. It forced me into an unwanted spotlight, and the humiliation was something I carried with me for years. Witnessing such an incident can also be profoundly unsettling for those who are there to see it, and it's a lasting reminder of the power and responsibility that adults hold over young minds.

Thankfully, during these trying times, I had two exceptional teachers who made a lasting impact on me: Mr. Shaw and Mr. Pass. I often wonder what became of them beyond the simple passage of time. They were beacons of hope in an otherwise challenging educational journey. Fourth grade was a year of transition and change for me. I was demoted out of the gifted class, a decision that stung, but I eventually found myself in Mr. Shaw's 5th-grade class. He was an African American teacher who didn't tolerate nonsense and had a deep passion for his calling. He introduced me to the art of writing, requiring us to pen short essays on a regular basis. It was through his guidance that I began to develop a love for writing. Those essays became a means of self-expression, a way to give voice to the thoughts and feelings I often kept hidden.

My journey with Mr. Shaw was initially marked by resistance. All the writing assignments he piled on us left me disgruntled. Writing essays seemed like a chore, but as time passed, something remarkable happened. I began to embrace the process, and my abilities began to shine. Mr. Shaw didn't just let it pass; he noticed my transformation and encouraged me to write even more.

I wasn't confined to writing alone. With Mr. Shaw's guidance and inspiration, my performance in various academic areas flourished that year. His unwavering belief in me propelled me to be my best. In the end, I was placed back into the gifted class for sixth grade, and it came with a command not to embarrass him – a testament to his faith in my potential.

But it wasn't just academic support that Mr. Shaw provided. He believed in me so much that he offered me and my brother scholarships for a summer day camp he oversaw. For the first time in my educational journey, I was no longer invisible. Someone saw me, truly saw me, and that someone believed in me, taking a genuine interest in my growth. It was a turning point, a sign of hope that ignited something within me. I didn't know exactly where this newfound hope would lead, but it felt different, and I liked it. This belief in myself and my abilities began shaping my journey, pushing me to do better in school and life.

Then there was Mr. Pass, our chorus teacher, a kind and gentle soul with a hippie-like demeanor. He, too, took a special interest in me. To this day, many of my college friends and others find it hard to believe that I used to possess the ability to sing. It's quite embarrassing, but it's a truth I hold dear.

I was born with a gift for singing, and I excelled as a second soprano. Mr. Pass recognized this talent and gave me solo parts in school performances. My most significant role was singing the lead in Sister Sledge's "We Are Family." I still remember every word, which is a feat considering my tendency to make up lyrics as I go. But even with all the attention and the solos, it wasn't enough to make me believe in me or in the power of my gift.

It's funny how self-doubt can overshadow the most extraordinary talents. Mr. Pass saw my potential, but I struggled to see it within myself. My voice was a treasure that I hadn't yet learned to cherish. These teachers, Mr. Shaw and Mr. Pass, showed me that my invisibility was not a definition of my worth but rather an overlooked part of my potential. They provided me with the encouragement and belief that would shape the path of my future, a path where I would learn to believe in myself and appreciate the gifts that I had been blessed with.

As I stepped into my teenage years, the shadow of self-doubt continued to loom over me. I began to play small, refusing opportunities and deflecting compliments under the guise of shyness. But deep down, it was a battle with feelings of inferiority and a sense of not being good enough. The label of "shy" became my shield, protecting me from the vulnerability of believing in my own worth.

Mr. Pass's belief in me had ignited a glimmer of hope, a ray that whispered, "You are seen, and you are valuable." It was a notion I clung to, a ray of light in a world that often felt dim. I began to believe that if Mr. Pass could see me, then perhaps others could see me, too.

In an effort to assimilate and feel more accepted, I struck up friendships with many of my white peers. The camaraderie I felt was comforting, yet I remained aware of the differences that set me apart. My white friends lived in nice houses, wore designer clothes, and experienced a level of privilege that was foreign to me. I had to worry about how to style my hair, what to wear, and navigate the world with a sensitivity to the unwritten rules.

I realized that to exist harmoniously in their world, I had to learn the art of invisibility. It meant engaging with my white friends in a non-confrontational manner so as not to intimidate them with my "magic melanin," as you aptly put it. This act of invisibility became a necessary survival strategy, a way to fit in without compromising who I was.

But then came puberty and the challenges of middle school, a time of transition and self-discovery, which proved to be a difficult phase for me. My white friends, or perhaps their parents, began to distance themselves from me, and it felt like a rejection. I started to resent my mother for putting me in a space where I didn't feel accepted by anyone. I felt caught between two worlds – not fully accepted at school, a significant part of my developmental journey, and not entirely embraced when I returned home at the end of the day.

Home, my supposed refuge, was where I was constantly teased. I was smart, talked differently, and had led a sheltered life compared to my friends, who were considered popular, pretty, and pursued by the boys. It was a painful contrast and persisted until I graduated from high school, solidifying my invisible theory as my reality.

These years were a mix of self-doubt, self-discovery, and the never-ending struggle to belong. I was on a quest to find my place in a world that often saw me through a narrow lens. It was a journey filled with lessons and challenges, eventually leading me to question the concept of invisibility and the possibility of breaking free from its grasp.

Chapter 6: Finding My Voice

What does discovering your voice mean? Is it true that discovering your voice helps you discover who you are and your life's ambition?

You want to fit in and be an asset to others. You want those around you to hear what you have to say. You want to be genuine and important.

It's not just the old you you discover when you rediscover your voice. Instead, you learn more about who you are. You have greater freedom to express yourself and be heard when you can discover your voice.

Have you discovered who you are? If you haven't already, consider the following: "What are the reasons behind your fear of speaking up?" and "Who are the voices or groups controlling your ability to speak?"

The important thing to remember is that writing or speaking is the first step in discovering your voice. You can tell someone sounds like you when you hear them speak or read your words. The first step to finding your voice is being able to speak with confidence.

Finding your voice is not about discovering something new within yourself; rather, it's about learning a little bit more of yourself. You have a bit more flexibility to express yourself, speak out, and be heard. Your voice is your truth. You discover that your voice can only be heard within you and no one else but yourself.

Finding your voice first starts with knowing that your voice is your truth. What is your truth? Your truth is the current emotion you are feeling at the moment. Your truth is your personal perspective on an issue or challenge you are dealing with. Your truth is the desire you have for yourself regarding your life, dreams, and goals. Your truth is your opinion on a subject matter. Your voice is the articulation of your truth in moments.

Over the years, I discovered my voice and became loud while still retaining my sense of decorum, responsibility, larger-than-life personality, fun nature, and intelligence. However, I always felt restricted in my ability to express myself fully. To be honest, I had a secret belief for many years that if I played small, I would be seen more and be accepted. I believed that if I allowed myself to be completely myself, nobody would like me, and I wouldn't be included in the circle of important people.

For many years, I lived a lie where I couldn't be quirky, corny, awkward, and goofy. I allowed myself to shrink and hide in the shadow of my peers whom I believed were better, more accomplished, prettier, accepted, and loved. Internally, I lived in a world behind others, but externally, no one could tell.

I have never shared this with anyone before, but I feel safe enough to do it now. You, my reader, are the first to witness my vulnerable state. Most of my friends would never believe this, as I always presented myself as strong and confident in my various social circles. But the truth is, I'm not always like that on the inside. I think many of us can relate to this - we've learned how to put on a good face, but our true emotions and feelings are often different. For me, I wanted to change that.

I wanted to be authentic, real, and confident both inside and out. I wanted to be big, bold, and true to myself without hiding behind a mask of fake confidence and bravado.

From a young age, I learned to be responsible and show up as strong, confident, and courageous. As the oldest child, I was often tasked with protecting my younger brother, so I had to push down any fears, insecurities, anxieties, or worries I had in order to ensure our safety and get us both home safely. It was a survival mechanism that taught me valuable lessons about resilience and determination.

As a "latchkey kid," I was responsible for locking the door behind me and my brother to ensure our safety while our parents were away. This term referred to children who carried a key around their necks to unlock and enter their homes alone. Growing up this way, I had to learn many things quickly, like standing up for myself and my brother when picked on and sometimes even fighting back. I had to develop the ability to not dwell on the hurtful words said to me and about me if I wanted to be accepted by my peers.

Growing up, I learned some valuable lessons simply by playing outside with my friends and feeling like part of my community. If I had taken all the hurtful words and actions to heart, I doubt I would have ever wanted to go outside again. Our surroundings have a significant impact on shaping who we are, and many of the messages I received during my childhood caused me to try and stay under the radar.

I believed that if I could make myself a little smaller, I would be less noticeable and avoid being called hurtful names. In fact, I once had a so-called best friend in middle school who told me that the only chance I had of dating someone was in the romance novels I constantly read.

I believe that she did not intend to say something so hurtful, and I do not think she realized how deeply her words affected me because, in a way, I agreed with her. During that period of my life, I did not receive any attention or validation from boys. As a matter of fact, they would tease me and provoke me to fight. During this time, I realized it was Jesus who got me through this phase of my life. I was extremely lonely because I felt no one else was experiencing what I was going through at that time. I harbored a secret pain shared by both me and my Lord. I refrained from confiding in anyone, fearing being perceived as weak or fragile. I did not want to burden my mother, who was already grappling with her own challenges as a single parent, tirelessly striving to provide a roof over our heads, food on the table, and clothing for me and my brothers. To cope with the overwhelming anguish and loneliness, I often resorted to sharp and disrespectful remarks, which adults referred to as a "fresh mouth."

I mastered the art of using sharp words and being defiant. Eventually, I mustered up the courage to curse, shutting down anyone who seemed to be a threat. Of course, my sharp words often got me into trouble, especially with my mother, but I refused to let go of my ability to speak my mind. Now, I use my words for good, to uplift and motivate, and to ignite a sense of greatness in those who can relate to my story.

Reflecting on both my childhood and my time in the corporate world, I realized that society often restricted me from being bold and ambitious. As a woman of African American descent with a deep complexion, I couldn't fully express my potential in corporate America either. To avoid intimidating my white colleagues, I learned how to interact with them in non-confrontational ways. For over 15 years, I toiled away in a realm where I felt both unseen and invisible. How is it possible to go to work every day yet feel completely unnoticed? In the corporate sphere, I made excuses for not excelling in my roles and leaned on microaggressions as a crutch. Ironically, it was in corporate America that I experienced the most invisibility, frustration, and stress.

No matter what I did, I never seemed to get the game right. However, I have witnessed numerous instances of other African American women who faced similar, if not more severe, microaggressions and still managed to succeed. I spent the majority of my fifteen years in corporate America utterly miserable. I felt miserable and invisible until one day, when I almost got fired. A client reached out to my superiors because of my blunt remarks, and I must have said something that deeply offended them. But then, there was a holy intervention! At the time, I had an African American leader who called me into her office and delivered a loving yet painful lecture that helped me turn things around. I went home feeling defeated and scared.

After all, I had a child who depended on me, and returning home to New York was not an option. I didn't know how to change my situation, but I humbled myself before God, and He revealed the way. He showed me that despite all the invisibility and microaggressions I faced, He had blessed me with this job and expected me to perform with excellence, humility, and gratitude.

Having to humble myself and let go of my justifications and excuses was a major turning point for me. However, I obeyed and did what was revealed to me. All glory to God; that was the defining moment in my life that completely changed its path. Not only did I manage to keep my job, but I also got promoted to a better position as a trainer and facilitator for learning and development, which set me up for the next steps in my career.

In this role, my manager, who I still deeply admire and remain connected to, arranged for me to pursue my Counseling degree while being financially supported by my employer. The rest is history. God places Some individuals in our lives to remind us that He sees us. Misty was that person for me—she saw me, believed in me, and helped me position myself for greater opportunities. It was at this junction in my journey things began to crystallize.

God has always seen me and was ordering my steps, paving the way, and making the crooked places straight. I have never gone unnoticed because the one who truly matters, My God, always sees me.

So, I didn't feel I could fully express myself at school or corporate America, but can you believe I couldn't express my true self even in the church? It was the one place where I thought I would be liberated to be my authentic self because of the incredible God I believed in. The one place where I thought I could come as I am and be completely embraced—well, I was mistaken in that assumption. I grew up in a church and, later in life, belonged to a church that taught one to follow a very conservative and narrow way of living, which I did for many years without questioning. However, I began to feel restricted, trapped, and inauthentic in my faith because of the expectations of the church leaders. I felt that I could not freely dance, listen to non-Christian music, or enjoy a glass of wine, even though I didn't drink and still don't. I needed to form my relationship with God and the Bible rather than just following the church's teachings.

I started to feel condemned for wanting to enjoy certain aspects of life and began to suppress my true personality, as I thought it would "call attention to myself."

For your relationship with God, I share this experience to help others understand that everyone's relationship with God can look different, and it's important to find what works for you.

There was also my personal life as a vibrant young woman who desired companionship. However, I felt apprehensive about being truly open in romantic relationships due to the fear of rejection. I downplayed my significance in personal relationships by tolerating disrespect and mediocrity, staying in situations when I should have left, all because I yearned for love and someone to share my life with. Eventually, I reached a point where I gave up and refrained from dating for many years while raising my daughter. I diminished myself once again, and my weight fluctuate, teetering towards the larger side, even though being overweight wasn't my natural body frame. I started dressing based on my weight and wearing clothes that didn't align with my authentic personality. The most crucial aspect was that I started to doubt the worthiness of experiencing true love or having a relationship beyond the one I had with my Creator.

I had to combat thoughts that I was unattractive, overweight, unsuccessful, and undesirable to the opposite sex. On countless nights, tears streamed down my face as loneliness engulfed me during what I consider my desert season. Would anyone ever truly see me and want to love me? Perhaps a companion was not meant for me, and I needed to find ways to accept this. Yet, I was completely mistaken, as I later realized that it simply wasn't my time; my delay was never a denial. There may have been one or two potential partners, but nothing noteworthy, as they either weren't supposed to be for me or weren't genuinely interested in me.

Playing small had become a way of life for me, deeply ingrained in my mindset, exerting a powerful hold. My perception of myself was fundamental to my decisions and my approach to life. Instead of seeing myself as invisible, a choice I had consistently made, I could have embraced the way God sees me. By relegating myself to invisibility, I unintentionally inflicted the most profound pain upon myself.

These lived experiences within my family, education, career, and faith community reinforced the belief that being big was not an option, compelling me to continue playing small. However, I now realize the significance of shedding this mindset and embracing a different narrative. It is time to step out of the shadows and embrace the possibilities that await.

Chapter 7: What Do You See?

We shape our self-perception through interactions with others, taking into consideration their responses to us and how they categorize us. However, it's important to note that their reactions may be influenced by their own biases, so we don't always receive an accurate reflection of ourselves.

Comparisons with others are inevitable despite our efforts to avoid them. We often compare ourselves to the expectations our friends and family set. Society also imposes roles and expectations, such as having a successful career or being a good parent, which contributes to our self-perception.

We continuously evaluate ourselves. A positive self-image leads to confidence and self-acceptance, while a negative self-image can result in feelings of inferiority and even depression. Those who develop a mature and realistic self-image are less affected by every critical comment.

Let's begin by discussing my perception of myself. It took me many years to realize that I am beautiful, inside and out. It took a lot of courage and self-love to be able to not only acknowledge this about myself but also express it in writing. It wasn't until I entered college and started attracting the attention of the opposite sex that I slowly began to realize that I am quite attractive.

If you recall, I mentioned earlier how I was subjected to harsh teasing and can still remember the hurtful words I was called. I was referred to as "Blackie" because of my darker skin tone and "bald-headed" because my hair was not considered long. However, I have always had hair; I have beautiful 4c hair that I didn't fully appreciate until the natural hair movement gained momentum.

I was called ugly and told that I had large lips, but in reality, my lips were full rather than big. Even if they were big, they were still perfectly fine, but these words influenced my perception of myself. As I later discovered, my lips are quite beautiful and alluring, and they would soon become desired by many, leading to a multi-billion-dollar industry due to full and even big lips being desired and sought after.

My hair was another aspect that contributed to shaping my self-perception, as I have always been fond of hair and received my first wig at the age of seven. My beloved grandmother, who was affectionately known as "Nonnie," gifted me this wig." Bless my mother's heart, she didn't quite know how to manage my hair. She used a Vigarol treatment on my hair, which is a less effective version of a perm that required constant upkeep; otherwise, your hair would fall out. Unfortunately, that is exactly what happened to my hair. This experience did not boost my self-confidence and only gave my neighborhood tormentors more ammunition to tease me. To add the finishing touch, I wasn't exactly the most stylishly dressed girl either, which contributed to more teasing. My mother faced financial difficulties, and buying me designer clothes was not a priority. However, making sure I had neat, clean, and presentable clothing was always on her mind. I mistakenly held resentment toward my mother because she couldn't afford to give me the same things my peers had. But she did her best and worked tirelessly so I could have what I needed.

Unfortunately, I allowed the words, opinions, and views of others to impact my self-perception and self-esteem. It took years of personal growth and renewing my mind through the guidance of God's Word to truly see myself and learn how to love who I am. I know that my journey of growth is ongoing and lifelong, and I must always put in the effort to sustain my progress.

To be completely honest, writing about this now evokes profound sadness and poses a challenge to be consistently authentic and transparent in ways I haven't experienced before. However, it also underscores the importance of this book. I know that I am not alone in my journey, and there are other people, particularly women from various ethnic backgrounds, who can relate and find solace in my story.

It took me a while to recognize my beauty, but I am proud to say that I am indeed pretty. The negative words and teasing I endured shaped my self-perception, but I have come to appreciate my unique features: dark complexion skin, full lips, and beautiful 4c hair. Though my self-appreciation took time, I have ultimately learned to embrace and celebrate my beauty.

Bullying can have a devastating impact on a person's self-image, especially when it is sustained over a long period of time. It can be difficult to break free from the negative messages that bullies instill in us, but it is possible. Here are some tips on how to build your self-image:

1. Identify your negative thoughts and beliefs.

The first step to building your self-image is to identify your negative thoughts and beliefs about yourself. This can be difficult, as these thoughts and beliefs may be so ingrained that you don't even realize you have them. However, it is important to identify these negative thoughts and beliefs to challenge them and replace them with more positive ones.

2. Challenge your negative thoughts and beliefs and reframe them with positive thoughts and beliefs.

Once you have identified your negative thoughts and beliefs, you can begin to challenge them. Ask yourself if there is any evidence to support these negative thoughts and beliefs. If not, try to replace them with more positive thoughts and beliefs. If you have negative thoughts about yourself, challenge them. For example, instead of thinking, *"I'm not good enough,"* think, *"I am capable and deserving."*

3. Focus on your strengths and accomplishments.

Your strengths are your superpower, and you want to ensure you excel and improve upon your strengths. Please make a list of your strengths and achievements and review it regularly. This will help you focus on the positive aspects of yourself and to boost your self-confidence.

4. Surround yourself with positive people.

Surround yourself with positive people who support you and make you feel good about yourself. Avoid spending time with people who are negative or who make you feel bad about yourself.

5. Seek professional help.

If you are struggling to build your self-image on your own, consider seeking professional help from a therapist or counselor. They can help you identify and challenge your negative thoughts and beliefs, develop positive coping mechanisms, and build self-confidence.

For instance, some people who carry memories of trauma and continue living their lives with unresolved trauma may be hesitant to seek help from a professional. If that is you, there are some things you can do to be more self-confident until you decide to seek professional help. Here are some additional tips:

6. Identify your strengths and weaknesses.

Everyone has strengths and weaknesses. It's important to identify your weaknesses so that you can focus on your strengths and work on improving them. Please make a list of your strengths and accomplishments and review it regularly. When you have self-confidence, you're more likely to take risks and go after your goals.

7. Set realistic goals.

When you set goals that are too difficult to achieve, you're setting yourself up for failure. This can damage your self-confidence. Instead, set small, achievable goals you can build on over time. As you achieve your goals, your self-confidence will grow.

8. Celebrate your successes.

Take the time to celebrate your successes, both big and small. This will help you to appreciate your accomplishments and build your self-confidence. When you achieve a goal, take some time to reflect on your success and be proud of yourself.

9. Take care of yourself.

When you take care of yourself, you show yourself that you value and respect yourself. Make sure to eat healthy foods, stay hydrated, get enough sleep, and exercise regularly. Taking care of your physical and mental health will help you to feel better about yourself. Building self-confidence takes time and effort, but it's worth it. When you have self-confidence, you're more likely to take risks and go after your goals.

Self-esteem is subject to change both daily and from moment to moment. There are moments when you have a strong feeling of self-worth and believe that nothing can ever defeat you.

Soon after, unfavorable ideas could start to fill your head. Perhaps after a great post, you feel your confidence increase as you browse around social media, but it quickly wanes.

This shift in your self-worth occurs many times daily, sometimes even at the same hour.

Daily effort is required to maintain a strong sense of self-worth. It could be draining. According to the American Psychological Association, having high self-esteem is key to positive mental health and well-being.

Having a healthy and high self-esteem contributes to the development of coping skills, which helps you during life challenges and adversity and puts negative situations in perspective.

10. Practice proper posture

Proper posture is a way to change your body language to make you feel more confident. When you stand or sit up straight, it relays an air of confidence and self-assuredness. Try standing up or sitting up straight with your shoulders back and your head held high. How does that slight shift in posture make you feel? It should make you feel more confident and assertive.

11. Affirm yourself

Affirmations are positive statements that you repeat to yourself to boost your self-confidence. For example, you could repeat affirmations such as "I am capable," "I am worthy," or "I am strong."

12. Visualize success

Visualization is a technique that you can use to imagine yourself achieving your goals and living a successful life. When you visualize success, you're training your mind to believe you can achieve anything you want. Remember, you are worthy of love, respect, and happiness. Believe in yourself and your abilities; you will be BIG and unstoppable.

Chapter 8: Big As External Perception

Embracing your "BIG" internally before projecting it externally is a powerful journey of self-realization. It's like building a skyscraper; you start by laying a strong foundation within yourself, fostering belief, confidence, and authenticity. This internal alignment becomes the cornerstone for the magnificent structure you present to the world.

Think of it as a personal metamorphosis, evolving from self-doubt to self-assurance. It's not just about portraying confidence on the surface but genuinely feeling it in your core. That depth of belief can resonate powerfully with others, creating a magnetic pull that draws them toward your authenticity.

Imagine this journey as a tapestry, each thread representing a moment where you reinforced your internal belief. Through acceptance and understanding of the time it takes to reach this point, you've woven a story of growth and resilience. That story becomes your unique narrative, guiding you as you step into your full "BIG" self.

Imagine life as a grand expedition, a breathtaking adventure rather than a sprint towards an elusive finish line. It's about relishing the scenery, the challenges, and the triumphs along the path while extending an open invitation to fellow travelers to join in this exhilarating odyssey.

In this expedition, you serve as both a seasoned guide and a compassionate companion. Your message echoes like a resounding beacon across the landscape of existence: "God sees you, I see you, and your presence is valued." It's like casting a spotlight on those who may have felt hidden in the shadows, illuminating their uniqueness and significance.

Picture yourself as an artist, brushing vibrant strokes onto a canvas of life, vividly capturing the beauty and diversity of everyone's "BIG." You don't just acknowledge it; you honor and celebrate it. Your canvas becomes a masterpiece, showcasing a mosaic of diverse stories, dreams, and potentials.

It's as if you've opened the door to a grand ballroom where everyone is welcome to dance and revel in their individuality. You're the conductor orchestrating a symphony of acceptance and celebration, where every note and participant contributes to the harmonious melody of existence.

I stand here not as a solitary figure but as a torchbearer for a collective movement—a movement rooted in the profound principles of self-love, acceptance, validation, and empowerment. It's as if we've formed an interconnected tapestry, where each thread represents an individual's journey, yet together, we weave a fabric of strength and resilience. In this journey toward self-discovery and acceptance, I extend my hand to you, not to lead but to walk alongside you. It's a partnership—a shared expedition into the depths of who you are. Together, we embark on a quest to unravel the intricacies of your being to uncover the treasures hidden within.

Imagine standing in front of a mirror, not just to see your reflection but also to understand the essence that truly defines you. I'm here to hold up that mirror, not to dictate what you should see, but to facilitate the exploration of your own reflection. While discovering what makes you uniquely "you," you'll find the seeds of empowerment and authenticity. Like an explorer mapping uncharted territories, I encourage you to venture into the landscapes of your soul. What are the valleys and peaks that shape your beliefs, your desires, and your fears? Together, let's navigate these terrains, unraveling the layers that have woven the intricate tapestry of your existence.

It's a journey of self-identification—an expedition into your own depths to understand, acknowledge, and honor what makes you extraordinary. You are a mosaic of experiences, dreams, passions, and quirks, and I am here as your ally, guiding you to embrace the full spectrum of who you are. Shall we chart the course together, navigating through the maze of self-discovery, acknowledging the beauty in your uniqueness, and uncovering the powerful essence that is inherently yours?

Who am I?

It's a question that echoes in the corridors of my mind, resonating with the essence of my being. I'm on a quest to decipher the intricate layers composing the tapestry of "me." Each thread tells a story—a tale of experiences, aspirations, beliefs, and passions interwoven into the fabric of my existence.

In this unfolding narrative, I'm not merely a static character but an evolving protagonist sculpted by the choices I make, the lessons I learn, and the dreams I chase. I'm becoming the architect of my own growth, shaping myself through introspection, resilience, and an unwavering commitment to authenticity.

What makes me, ME? It's the amalgamation of my quirks, passions, fears, and aspirations. It's the rhythm of my heartbeat synchronized with the symphony of my thoughts. The kaleidoscope of experiences has painted the canvas of my life, creating a mosaic that is uniquely mine.

Yet, this journey of self-discovery isn't solely about unraveling the mysteries of my identity. It's equally about embracing and loving what I discover. Self-love and acceptance are the nurturing waters that allow the seeds of authenticity to bloom.

So, how do I demonstrate this profound self-love and acceptance? It starts with embracing imperfection, acknowledging that within these imperfections lie the beauty of my individuality. It's about practicing self-compassion, offering myself the same kindness and understanding I would extend to a dear friend facing challenges.

Another aspect is cultivating gratitude—a daily ritual of acknowledging the blessings in my life, including the uniqueness that defines me. Self-care has become a cornerstone, not just physical but also nurturing my mental and emotional well-being.

To harness self-love and acceptance is to live authentically, align my actions with my values, set healthy boundaries, and celebrate my accomplishments, no matter how small.

As I navigate this path of self-discovery and acceptance, I'm eager to explore my BIG—the essence that makes me stand out, the unique blend of talents, passions, and perspectives I bring to the world. I yearn to embrace it fully, allowing it to shine brightly and positively impact the lives of those around me.

Ask yourself: Who are you at your core? Who do you envision yourself becoming? What defines your uniqueness? Once you unearth your essence, how do you cultivate self-love and acceptance? How can you magnify and honor your uniqueness, your 'BIG,' in the world?

I'm here to help you explore new ways of living life — ways you might not have thought of yet. Let's dive into exciting opportunities that can make your dreams come alive. It's about trying new things, finding what you're good at, and saying yes to what makes you truly happy.

And when you start living this bigger life, don't keep it to yourself! Share the joy! Your experience can be a light for someone else. Tell your story and inspire others to embrace who they are and go after what they want.

Joining the Be BIG collective isn't just an invite; it's a warm welcome. It's a community where everyone's voice matters and where we cheer each other on. It's about turning up the happiness dial for yourself and for anyone looking for a boost of confidence and realness.

So, will you be part of this movement? Will you share your story, your joy, and your journey with us? Let's spread inspiration and positivity, touching lives and making a difference. I'd love for you to join me on this amazing journey!

Take a moment to answer these questions.

Who are you, really?

Think about it for a moment. What defines you at your core? What experiences, beliefs, and passions shape your identity?

Who are you becoming?

Picture yourself in the future. What kind of person do you aspire to be? What qualities and values do you want to embody as you evolve?

Where do you see yourself in the next five years?

Envision your future. What does success and fulfillment look like to you? What kind of life do you hope to be living in five years?

What are some things you can do to show yourself love and acceptance?

Consider this: How do you treat yourself? Are you kind to yourself, especially in tough times? What steps can you take to prioritize your well-being and embrace your uniqueness?

Reflecting on these questions can be a powerful way to gain insight into yourself and set a course toward a more fulfilling and authentic life.

Chapter 9: BIG as an Internal Perception

Your belief system plays a pivotal role in shaping your life's trajectory. If you harbor negative beliefs about the concept of "big," envisioning a life of abundance, boldness, and limitless possibilities becomes a distant dream. However, it's crucial to recognize that there is no inherent judgment in choosing a different path. Ultimately, you have the autonomy to define and design the life that resonates with your deepest aspirations.

This book is an empowering guide for those who have consciously chosen to embrace a BIG life, one where they take ownership of their dreams and forge their own path, unfettered by societal expectations or limiting beliefs. Embracing a BIG life requires a fundamental shift in perspective, a belief that living large and pursuing your passions is not only possible but also deeply fulfilling.

The Inseparable Triad: Belief, Faith, and Hope

At the heart of this transformation lies the inseparable triad of belief, faith, and hope. Belief forms the foundation upon which your aspirations rest. It's the unwavering conviction that you possess the capacity to achieve your goals, no matter how audacious they may seem.

Faith, the unwavering trust in something beyond yourself, fuels your journey. The belief in a higher power, a guiding force, or an inner strength empowers you to persevere through challenges and setbacks.

Hope, the optimistic anticipation of a positive outcome, sustains you along the way. It's the belief that your efforts will yield desired results and that your dreams are not mere fantasies but attainable realities.

Cultivating a Positive Belief in BIG

To fully embrace a BIG life, cultivating a positive belief in its essence is paramount. This entails shedding negative self-talk and replacing it with empowering affirmations that reinforce your capabilities. Surround yourself with like-minded individuals who share your vision and encourage you to reach for the stars.

Engage in activities that ignite your passion and fuel your enthusiasm. Seek out mentors who have walked the path you aspire to tread, drawing inspiration from their experiences and wisdom.

God only requires that you have

"Faith is the size of a mustard seed, and you can move mountains."

-Matthew 17: 20-21.

In Mark 9:23, Jesus shares that.

"If you can believe, all things are possible to those who believe."

An explanation of the passages from Matthew 17:20-21 and Mark 9:23:

The Power of Faith

In these passages, Jesus emphasizes the transformative power of faith. He uses two metaphors, the mustard seed, and the moving mountains, to illustrate that even the smallest amount of faith can accomplish extraordinary things.

Faith the Size of a Mustard Seed

A mustard seed is one of the smallest seeds known to humankind. Yet, Jesus asserts that if you have faith as small as a mustard seed, you can move mountains. This metaphorical comparison highlights the immense power that faith, even in its smallest form, can wield.

Moving Mountains

Moving mountains is a symbolic representation of overcoming seemingly insurmountable obstacles. It signifies the ability to achieve the improbable, to break through barriers, and to achieve what may appear impossible.

All Things Are Possible to Those Who Believe

In Mark 9:23, Jesus reiterates the transformative power of faith by declaring that "all things are possible to those who believe." This statement emphasizes the limitless potential that faith unlocks. It suggests that with unwavering faith, no challenge is too great, no dream too ambitious.

The Essence of Faith

The underlying message in these passages is not about the literal ability to move mountains or achieve anything physically impossible. Rather, it's about the transformative power of faith to shape our perception of possibilities and empower us to overcome perceived limitations.

Faith as an Enabler

Faith serves as an enabler, allowing us to tap into our inner strength, resilience, and determination. It motivates us to persevere, to push boundaries, and to believe in the potential for extraordinary outcomes.

The Role of Belief

Faith is closely intertwined with belief. Belief is the foundation upon which faith rests. It's the unwavering conviction in something, whether it's a higher power, a personal aspiration, or an overarching belief in the power of the human spirit.

Faith and Belief in Action

When faith and belief are combined with action, they become a potent force for personal transformation and achieving extraordinary results. Faith empowers us to believe in the impossible, while belief motivates us to act and make that impossible a reality.

The Empowering Choice to Believe: Unleashing Your Potential

In his statement, "If you can believe," Jesus places the onus of belief squarely on the individual. He doesn't say, "When you believe," implying that belief is a passive phenomenon that happens to you. Instead, he emphasizes the active nature of belief, the power of choice that lies within each of us.

This empowering message highlights that the key to unlocking extraordinary possibilities lies within our own hands. The magic lies not in some external force or spiritual intervention but in the transformative power of our own beliefs.

The Choice to Believe: A Catalyst for Transformation

The choice to believe is not a mere intellectual exercise; it's a transformative decision that has the power to reshape our lives. When we choose to believe, we tap into a reservoir of strength, resilience, and determination that lies dormant within us.

This belief empowers us to overcome perceived limitations, push boundaries, and pursue our aspirations with unwavering determination. It's the fuel that ignites our passion, propels us forward, and enables us to achieve remarkable feats.

The Power of Belief: Unleashing the Impossible

Jesus' statement, "All things are possible to you if you choose to believe," underscores the limitless potential that unfolds when we embrace belief. It's a reminder that no dream is too ambitious, and no challenge too daunting when we harness the power of belief.

This belief empowers us to see possibilities where others see obstacles to envision success where others anticipate failure. It allows us to approach challenges with confidence, knowing that we possess the inner strength to overcome them.

What Do You Have to Lose?

The choice to believe is not without its risks. It requires us to step outside our comfort zones, embrace the possibility of failure, and face the fear of the unknown. However, the potential rewards far outweigh the risks.

When we choose to believe, we open ourselves up to a world of possibilities, a life filled with passion, purpose, and extraordinary achievements. We become the authors of our own destinies, shaping our lives with the power of belief. So, what do you have to lose? Embrace the power of choice, choose to believe, and unleash the extraordinary potential that lies within you.

Living a BIG life, one that is authentic, passionate, and impactful, requires a tremendous amount of courage. It's about stepping outside your comfort zone, embracing vulnerability, and pursuing your dreams despite the fear that may hold you back.

As a licensed therapist, I've witnessed firsthand how many individuals attempt to suppress their emotions, believing that denying them will bring peace. However, this approach is futile and detrimental to our overall well-being. Emotions, in all their forms, carry valuable information about our inner state, guiding our thoughts, behaviors, and relationships.

Suppressing emotions is like trying to constipate your body's natural processes. It leads to a buildup of unprocessed energy, manifesting as stress, anxiety, irritability, and a decreased tolerance for challenges. Instead of suppressing our emotions, we must learn to embrace them, to acknowledge their presence, and to understand the messages they convey.

When we allow ourselves to feel our emotions, even those that are uncomfortable, like fear, anxiety, or sadness, we create space for them to pass through.

We acknowledge their existence without letting them control us. It's important to remember that fear is not a sign of weakness; it's a natural human response to perceived threats. Fear and anxiety's purpose is to protect us, to signal that something may be dangerous. However, when we allow fear to paralyze us, it prevents us from pursuing our passions, fulfilling our potential, and living life to the fullest.

The courage to live BIG lies in acknowledging your fears, understanding their roots, and taking action despite them. It's about moving forward, not in the absence of fear, but in spite of it.

Your fears are not meant to hold you back; they are meant to be confronted, understood, and overcome. They are designed to test your resolve, to strengthen your determination, and to propel you towards your true purpose.

As a girl, around eight years old, I remember having to walk home with my brother from the bus stop through the projects. It was a long and scary walk, especially in the winter months when it got dark early. The towering apartment buildings seemed to close in on us, and I always imagined someone lurking in the shadows, ready to jump out and grab us.

Sometimes, the elevator was out of order, and we had to take the stairs to our third-floor apartment. The stairs were even scarier than the alleyways because they were so dark and echoey. I could hear every creak and groan of the old building, and I was always convinced that someone was following us up the stairs.

But even though I was scared, I never let my fears show. I knew my mother was counting on me to get my brother home safely, and I didn't want to disappoint her. So, I would grit my teeth and walk as fast as I could, ignoring the shadows, noises, and fear that were always gnawing at me.

It wasn't easy, but I eventually got used to the walk home from the bus stop. I learned to ignore my fears and focus on getting my brother home safely. And I learned that even when I was scared, I could still be brave.

Those walks home from the bus stop taught me a lot about myself. They taught me that I was stronger than I thought I was. They taught me that I could face my fears and come out on the other side. And they taught me that I was never alone. My mother was always there for me, even when I couldn't see her.

In the absence of other options, I became the sole solution for ensuring my brother's safe return home. I'm certain that if my mother had other alternatives, she would have gladly embraced them. She made numerous attempts to seek assistance from relatives, neighbors, and friends, but to no avail.

Cell phones were nonexistent during my childhood, and tracking devices were undoubtedly absent, leaving my mother with no way to assuage her anxieties about our safe return home. We were obliged to trust that our return would follow our departure from home in the morning, and we always did.

I share this experience with the hope that, even if it differs from your own, the underlying essence resonates with you. I am confident that you have encountered life experiences that instilled fear, anxiety, and worry within you. However, you somehow managed to conquer your inner demons, even if you were unaware of it.

The essence of living BIG lies in transcending the limitations imposed by fear, insecurity, and the relentless pursuit of external validation. It's about shedding the shackles of self-doubt, embracing our authenticity, and boldly pursuing our passions, regardless of the opinions or expectations of others.

Life itself is a BIG and precious gift, a fragile yet resilient tapestry of experiences, connections, and possibilities. Not everyone is fortunate enough to experience the full spectrum of life's offerings, yet you have been granted this extraordinary opportunity. We have just emerged from one of the most devastating pandemics in human history, a global crisis that claimed the lives of millions. The fact that you are reading this book and that you have survived and emerged from this ordeal is a testament to your resilience and the inherent strength that lies within you.

Given the fragility and preciousness of life, why settle for mediocrity, for playing it small? Technology may have shrunk the world in terms of connectivity, but the vastness of our planet and the cosmos it inhabits remains unchanged.

To truly flow in harmony with this grand existence, we must embrace our BIG potential, shedding the limitations that hinder our personal growth and fulfillment.

The Journey to BIG: Confronting Hindrances and Embracing Authenticity

The path to living BIG requires a willingness to confront the internal and external forces that hold us back. It's about identifying and eliminating the barriers that prevent us from fully embracing our potential.

What hindrances need to be removed from your life? Are you tethered to self-doubt, perpetually questioning your abilities and worth? Do you seek validation from external sources, constantly striving to meet the expectations of others rather than following your own compass?

These internal and external limitations serve as shackles, preventing us from soaring to our true heights. To live BIG, we must break free from these constraints, embracing our authenticity and the unique talents that lie dormant within us.

Letting Go: Shedding the Weight of the Past

Sometimes, the path to BIG requires letting go of things or people that no longer serve us. It's about releasing the weight of the past, the burdens that weigh us down and prevent us from moving forward.

Are you clinging to relationships that drain your energy and hinder your growth? Are you holding onto past failures, allowing them to dictate your present and future?

Letting go doesn't imply weakness; it's a courageous act of self-preservation, a decision to prioritize your well-being and personal growth. It's about creating space for new possibilities, relationships that nurture and uplift, and experiences that ignite your passion and propel you toward your dreams.

Living BIG is not passive; it requires active participation and a conscious decision to step outside your comfort zone and embrace the limitless possibilities that lie before you.

What will it take for you to show up BIG? What fears need to be confronted? What burdens need to be released?

The answers lie within you, waiting to be discovered. Embark on a journey of self-discovery, explore the depths of your potential, and unleash the extraordinary force that lies dormant within you.

Living BIG is not about seeking external validation or achieving societal norms; it's about living authentically, pursuing your passions with unwavering determination, and profoundly impacting the world around you. It's about embracing the limitless possibilities that lie within you and creating a life that is truly BIG in every sense of the word.

Chapter 10: Defining BIG

Living BIG is not merely a collection of grand gestures or extraordinary achievements; it's a mindset, a conscious decision to embrace the fullness of your existence and profoundly impact the world around you.

It's about accepting yourself wholeheartedly and recognizing the inherent goodness and potential instilled in you by your Creator. It's about understanding that your presence in this world is not merely a coincidence but a holy orchestration, a calling to live a life of purpose and significance.

Living BIG extends beyond personal fulfillment; it encompasses our relationships, our contributions to our communities, and the impact we leave on those entrusted to our care. It's about showing up authentically, passionately, and with unwavering commitment in every aspect of our lives.

This concept may seem daunting, a departure from the comfort of mediocrity and the pursuit of societal norms. However, I am here to guide you on this transformative journey, to equip you with strategies that will empower you to live BIG and make a remarkable difference in every area of your life.

Defining BIG: A Multifaceted Concept

BIG is not a one-dimensional concept; it encompasses a multitude of facets that contribute to a fulfilling and impactful existence.

- **Authenticity:** Living BIG begins with embracing your true self, shedding the masks and personas that may have hindered your personal growth. It's about aligning your actions with your values, expressing your thoughts and emotions with honesty, and living a life that is true to your core.

- **Passion:** Passion is the fuel that ignites our enthusiasm and propels us forward. Living BIG requires identifying your passions, the activities that set your soul on fire, and pursuing them with unwavering determination.

- **Purpose:** Purpose provides direction and meaning to our lives. Living BIG entails discovering your purpose, the unique contribution you are meant to make to the world, and aligning your actions with that purpose.

- **Impact:** Living BIG is not about personal glory; it's about positively impacting the world around you. It's about making a difference in the lives of others, contributing to your community, and leaving a legacy that will endure beyond your lifetime.

Embrace Your BIG Potential: A Transformative Journey

Embracing your BIG potential is not a destination but an ongoing journey of self-discovery, growth, and transformation. It requires consistent effort, a willingness to step outside your comfort zone, and a commitment to personal evolution.

- **Self-Discovery:** Embark on a journey of self-exploration, uncovering your strengths, talents, and unique perspectives. Understand your values, your passions, and the causes that resonate with you.

- **Personal Growth:** Continuously strive to expand your knowledge, develop new skills, and enhance your abilities. Embrace challenges as growth opportunities and seek mentors and guides who can support your journey.

- **Transformative Experiences:** Engage in activities that push you beyond your comfort zone, expose you to new perspectives, and challenge your assumptions. Travel to new places, engage in diverse cultures, and immerse yourself in experiences that broaden your understanding of the world.

Show Up BIG: Making a Difference

Living BIG is not about self-aggrandizement; it's about using your unique gifts and talents to positively impact the world.

- **Relationships:** Nurture meaningful relationships with family, friends, and community members. Be a source of support, encouragement, and inspiration to those around you.

- **Community Engagement:** Actively participate in your community, identify areas where your skills and talents can be utilized, and contribute to the betterment of your surroundings.

- **Mentorship:** Share your knowledge and experiences with others, providing guidance and support to those seeking personal and professional growth.

- **Global Citizenship:** Expand your awareness of global issues, advocate for causes that resonate with you, and contribute to the betterment of the world at large.

Defining BIG: A Spectrum of Meanings

The word "BIG" carries a multitude of meanings, each facet contributing to a comprehensive understanding of its significance. It's not merely a quantitative term denoting size or extent; it encapsulates a range of qualities that embody greatness, importance, and impact.

Size and Extent: The Tangible Dimension of BIG

In its most basic sense, "BIG" signifies considerable size, extent, or intensity. It refers to physically large or grand things, whether it's a towering skyscraper, a vast expanse of ocean, or a massive crowd of people. This physical magnitude often translates into a sense of awe and wonder, reminding us of the vastness and grandeur of the world around us.

Importance and Seriousness: The Weight of BIG

Beyond its physical dimensions, "BIG" also conveys a sense of importance and seriousness. It refers to matters with significant implications, holding gravitas and demanding attention. A "BIG" decision is one that carries substantial weight, influencing the course of events or affecting the lives of many.

Quality, Number, and Amount: The Abundance of BIG

The concept of "BIG" extends beyond physical size to encompass quality, number, and amount. It refers to things that are exceptional, outstanding, or plentiful. A "BIG" idea is one that is groundbreaking, innovative, and has the potential to revolutionize an industry or field of thought. A "BIG" personality is one that is charismatic and influential and leaves a lasting impression.

Enthusiasm, Interest, and Activity: The Vibrancy of BIG

"BIG" also signifies enthusiasm, interest, and activity. It refers to things that are done with passion, vigor, and a wholehearted commitment. A "BIG" fan is devoted and enthusiastically supports their team or artist. A "BIG" dreamer has bold aspirations, daring to envision and pursue grand ambitions.

Chief, Preeminent, and Imposing: The Significance of BIG

The word "BIG" is also used to denote chief, preeminent, and imposing qualities. It refers to things of the utmost importance, standing out as exceptional or superior. A "BIG" breakthrough is one that represents a significant advancement, opening new possibilities and shaping the future.

As an Adverb: The Extent of BIG

When used as an adverb, "BIG" means to a large amount or extent. It signifies a considerable degree or magnitude. "He won BIG" implies a significant victory, while "She laughed BIG" suggests a hearty and unrestrained expression of joy.

As a Noun: The Power and Influence of BIG

As a noun, "BIG" refers to an individual or organization of outstanding importance or power. It signifies a dominant player in a particular field or industry. "The BIG companies" are those that hold significant market share and exert considerable influence.

In conclusion, the word "BIG" encompasses a rich tapestry of meanings, reflecting its multifaceted nature. It signifies physical size, importance, quality, enthusiasm, and power, each dimension contributing to its overall essence. Whether used as an adjective, adverb, or noun, "BIG" consistently conveys a sense of greatness, impact, and significance.

The provided definitions of BIG heavily emphasize physical size, quantity, intensity, and capacity. These attributes, while significant, represent a limited perspective on what it truly means to be BIG.

My thoughts on these definitions are that they capture an important aspect of BIG but fail to encompass the deeper essence of what it means to live BIG. BIG is not merely about physical size or the accumulation of things; it's about the impact we make on the world, the connections we forge with others, and the legacy we leave behind.

My feelings regarding these definitions are that they are somewhat narrow and incomplete. They paint a picture of BIG that is focused on external measures and achievements, overlooking the internal qualities that make someone truly BIG.

When I examine these definitions in my life, I realize that they don't fully represent who I am or what I aspire to be. My physical size, material possessions, or position in society do not define me. I believe that my "BIGNESS" lies in my ability to connect with others, inspire and uplift those around me, and make a positive difference in the world.

The statement, "BIG is BIG because it not only is BIG, looks BIG, but feels BIG," resonates deeply with me. It captures the essence of BIG that goes beyond mere size and quantity. It's about having a presence, radiating energy and passion, and making an impact that is deeply felt by others.

I believe that everyone has the potential to live BIG, regardless of their physical size or socioeconomic status. "BIGNESS" is not about competing with others or achieving external validation; it's about embracing our true selves, pursuing our passions with unwavering determination, and positively impacting the world around us.

When we live BIG, we tap into a wellspring of inner strength, resilience, and determination. We become a beacon of inspiration, motivating others to pursue their own dreams and make their mark on the world.

The concept of BIG can indeed be intimidating, especially when associated with notions of grandeur and ambition. However, it's crucial to remember that

BIG is not a one-size-fits-all definition; it's a deeply personal journey of self-discovery and growth.

As I aptly pointed out, the acronym "BE BIG" serves as a reminder of the qualities that empower us to live BIG lives:

Boundless: Unfettered by limitations, embracing the limitless possibilities that lie before us.

Empowered: Possessing the inner strength and authority to pursue our passions and make a difference.

Bodacious: Exuding excellence, demonstrating remarkable talent and achievements.

Intuitive: Guided by our inner wisdom, tapping into the depths of our understanding.

Grandiose: Not in the sense of pretentiousness or self-aggrandizement, but in the sense of setting ambitious goals and making a profound impact.

The inclusion of the word "Grandiose" might initially raise concerns about its negative connotations. However, reframing the meaning in the context of living BIG is essential.

In this sense, Grandiose represents the audacity to dream big and the courage to pursue aspirations that may seem daunting to others. It's about embracing the extraordinary potential that lies within us and setting our sights on making a significant impact on the world. My decision to leave "Grandiose" in the acronym stems from my profound connection to a BIG and Grandiose God. Recognizing the holy source of your inspiration and the limitless possibilities that this connection unleashes reaffirms the positive essence of the word.

Living BIG is not about imitating others or conforming to societal expectations; it's about discovering your unique definition of BIG and pursuing it with unwavering determination. It's about tapping into your boundless potential, embracing your empowered spirit, and making a bodacious impact on the world.

So, embrace your intuitive wisdom, set grandiose goals, and fearlessly pursue your BIG dreams. Allow the acronym "BE BIG" to serve as a guiding beacon, illuminating the path toward a life of purpose, fulfillment, and extraordinary impact.

Reclaiming BIG: Overcoming Negative Perceptions and Embracing Your True Potential

The concept of "BIG" often evokes mixed emotions, with some embracing it as a source of inspiration and others viewing it with suspicion or even aversion. It's crucial to examine these perceptions and understand the underlying biases and judgments that may be clouding our understanding of what it truly means to live BIG.

Before embarking on this journey of self-discovery, acknowledge and address any negative connotations associated with the word "BIG." These perceptions may stem from past experiences, societal conditioning, or personal interpretations of the word.

Questioning Your Biases

Consider the following questions to identify your biases around the word "BIG":

- Do you associate BIG with arrogance, boastfulness, or self-aggrandizement?
- Do you perceive BIG individuals as pretentious or out of touch with reality?
- Do you believe that pursuing BIG goals is unnecessary or unrealistic?

Tracing the Origins of Your Perceptions

Reflect on the sources of your negative perceptions of "BIG":

- Did you witness instances where "BIG" was expressed in an excessive or inappropriate way?
- Were you ever discouraged from pursuing your own BIG dreams, leading to a sense of doubt or fear?

- Did you internalize societal messages that equated "MY BIG BEING" with negativity or undesirable traits?

Redefining BIG: A Personal Transformation

As you delve into these introspective questions, begin to reshape your understanding of "BIG" by:

- Separating "BIG" from Ego: Recognize that it is not about self-aggrandizement but about making a positive impact and living a life of purpose.

- Appreciating the Power of BIG Dreams: Embrace the audacity to dream big, understanding that ambitious goals can fuel personal growth and meaningful contributions.

- Acknowledging Diverse Expressions of "BIG": It manifests in various forms, from personal achievements to acts of kindness and community engagement.

Embracing Your BIG Potential

The realization that "BIG" is a way of life rather than a mere label opens doors to limitless possibilities:

- **Living with Passion and Purpose:** Pursue your passions with unwavering determination, aligning your actions with a sense of purpose and meaning.

- **Making a Positive Impact:** Strive to leave a positive mark on the world, whether through personal interactions, professional endeavors, or community engagement.

- **Inspiring Others to Dream BIG:** Share your enthusiasm and inspire others to embrace their own BIG dreams, creating a ripple effect of positive change.

Remember, living BIG is not about achieving external validation or conforming to societal norms; it's about embracing your authentic self, pursuing your passions with unwavering determination, and profoundly impacting the world around you. It's about recognizing the immense potential that lies within you and unleashing it to create a life that is truly BIG in every sense of the word.

Chapter 11: How To Be Big?

Playing small, dimming our inner light, and shrinking ourselves to fit into someone else's perception of "acceptable" is a familiar struggle for many. My story resonates with many who have chosen to downsize their authentic selves.

We often convince ourselves that playing small will shield us from the sting of rejection. We believe that blending in, conforming to expectations, and suppressing our true potential will make us more palatable to others. We fear that expressing our true selves, unique talents, and ambitions will make us stand out and become targets of criticism or exclusion.

In your case, I mention the presence of a "BIGNESS" within you, a yearning to break free from the confines of self-imposed limitations. This represents your authentic self, your full potential waiting to be unleashed. However, the fear of rejection holds you back, prompting you to shrink yourself to feel accepted.

The belief that playing small leads to belonging is a clever illusion. While it may provide a temporary sense of comfort and inclusion, it ultimately robs us of the opportunity to experience authentic connections and build genuine relationships.

Here's why playing small can be detrimental:

- **It limits your personal growth:** By suppressing your authentic self, you limit your potential for growth and development. You deny yourself the opportunity to explore your true desires and talents, ultimately hindering your ability to reach your full potential.

- **It hinders authentic relationships:** When you play small, you build relationships based on a facade rather than on your true self. This creates shallow connections that lack depth and genuine understanding.

- **It perpetuates the cycle of fear:** By constantly seeking validation and approval, you remain trapped in a cycle of fear and insecurity. This can manifest as anxiety, self-doubt, and a lack of confidence.

Breaking free from the habit of playing small requires courage, self-awareness, and a willingness to challenge your limiting beliefs. Here are some steps you can take:

- **Identify your limiting beliefs:** Start by recognizing the thoughts and beliefs that hold you back from expressing your true self. Are you afraid of criticism? Do you believe you're not good enough? Challenge these beliefs and replace them with self-affirmations that empower you.

- **Embrace your "BIGNESS":** Reconnect with that inner voice, the essence of your true self.

Acknowledge your unique talents and gifts and celebrate your individuality.

- **Seek authentic connections:** Surround yourself with people who appreciate and accept you for who you are. Cultivate relationships with individuals who inspire you to grow and encourage you to shine brightly.

- **Embrace vulnerability:** Allow yourself to be seen and heard, even if it means risking rejection. Remember, authentic connections are built on vulnerability and honesty.

- **Focus on your own journey:** Stop comparing yourself to others. Focus on your own unique path and celebrate your own achievements.

The journey of reclaiming it is an ongoing process. There will be moments of doubt and fear, but remember that you are worthy of love, acceptance, and belonging just as you are. By choosing to express your authentic self, you empower yourself and inspire others to do the same. You become a sign, showing others that it's okay to be BIG, to shine brightly, and to take up space in this world.

The fear of playing small often stems from the misconception that there is limited space for success, recognition, and belonging. This distorted thinking leads us to believe that we must compete with others, dimming our light to allow others to shine. However, the reality is that the world is abundant. Everyone has enough room to pursue their passions, make their mark, and contribute to the greater good.

Another limiting belief is that "Being Big" is reserved for extroverted personalities. While extroverts may feel naturally comfortable expressing themselves outwardly, introverts possess unique strengths that contribute significantly to the world. Introverts are often deeply introspective and thoughtful and possess a strong sense of self-awareness. These qualities are invaluable in any pursuit, and living BIG is no exception.

Being BIG as an introvert means:

- **Owning your unique voice:** You don't need to be the loudest in the room to make a difference. Regardless of your volume, your voice, perspective, and insights have value.

- **Leveraging your strengths:** Introverts excel at critical thinking, creative problem-solving, and deep reflection. Utilize these strengths to impact your chosen field or area of interest positively.

- **Finding your own way to shine:** You don't have to conform to extroverted expectations of leadership or influence. Find ways to express your "BIGNESS" that is authentic and energizing for you.

- **Building meaningful relationships:** Introverts often form deep and lasting connections with individuals. Use your ability to build strong relationships to create a network of support and collaboration.

Here are some tips for introverts to embrace their "BIG BEING":

- **Focus on your inner world:** Spend time reflecting on your values, passions, and goals. This self-awareness will guide you in making choices aligned with your authentic self.

- **Seek out like-minded individuals:** Connect with other introverts who share your values and aspirations. This will create a supportive environment where you can feel comfortable expressing your "BIGNESS."

- **Find your platform:** Whether it's through writing, speaking, or creative expression, find ways to share your ideas and make a difference in the world.

- **Set boundaries and protect your energy:** Introverts need time to recharge. Be mindful of your energy levels and set boundaries to avoid feeling depleted.

- **Celebrate your unique gifts:** Remember that your introversion is a strength, not a weakness. Embrace your individuality and use it to make a truly BIG impact.

Embracing your "BIGNESS" is a journey of self-discovery, shedding the masks and limitations that hinder your authentic expression. It's about recognizing that there is no "right" way to be BIG and that your individuality is your greatest asset.

This journey begins with introspection, asking yourself:

What thoughts are keeping you from being BIG?

These thoughts might be rooted in fear, self-doubt, or limiting beliefs. They could be whispering things like:

- "I'm not good enough."
- "I'm not qualified."
- "Who am I to dream so big?"
- "I don't want to stand out."
- "I'm afraid of rejection."

Identify these negative thoughts and challenge their validity. Replace them with empowering affirmations like:

- "I am worthy and capable."
- "I have unique talents and gifts to share."
- "I am worthy of achieving my dreams."
- "My voice matters."
- "I can handle challenges and setbacks."

What character flaws are preventing you from living BIG?

Sometimes, character flaws can act as roadblocks to "BEING BIG." These might include:

- **Procrastination:** Putting things off and delaying action can hinder your progress and prevent you from achieving your goals.

- **Fear of failure:** The fear of failing can paralyze you and keep you from taking risks and pursuing your dreams.

- **Perfectionism:** Striving for perfectionism can lead to self-doubt and dissatisfaction, hindering your ability to move forward.

- **Negative self-talk:** Engaging in negative self-talk can chip away at your confidence and limit your potential.

- **Lack of self-discipline:** Difficulty managing time and staying focused can derail your efforts and prevent you from reaching your goals.

Identifying and understanding these character flaws is the first step toward overcoming them. Seek resources and support systems to help you develop positive habits and overcome your weaknesses.

What changes can you make right now to help you get on course to your BIG?

Imagine this: you spend years nurturing a garden, meticulously tending to each seedling, shielding it from harsh weather, and providing it with every nutrient it needs. But what happens when you realize your love and care have inadvertently stunted its growth, preventing it from reaching its full potential?

This was the harsh realization I faced as a mother. With the best intentions, I had created a safe, controlled environment for my daughter, unknowingly limiting her opportunities to learn, grow, and discover her own "BIG BEING."

I shielded her from minor inconveniences, arranged her schedule around mine, and watched every step she took. I convinced myself I was protecting her, but I was teaching her to be small. I was projecting my own fears and anxieties onto her, preventing her from developing the independence and resilience she needed to flourish in the world.

The turning point came when my daughter, on the cusp of adulthood, received the key to our house. It was a seemingly insignificant gesture, but it represented a monumental shift in our dynamic. It was a tangible symbol of my trust in her ability to be responsible, navigate her own world, and face challenges. Letting go was not easy. It meant confronting my own fears and insecurities, learning to trust my daughter's judgment, and accepting that she would make mistakes, as we all do. But with each step toward her independence, I witnessed her "BIGNESS" blossom. She learned to navigate public transportation, handle unexpected situations, and make decisions based on her own values. She discovered a strength and confidence I had never known she possessed.

My journey from overprotection to empowerment has been a humbling one. It has taught me that true love doesn't seek to control but to empower. It means allowing my child to fall, pick herself up, and learn from her experiences. It means trusting her to find her own way, even if it leads her down paths I wouldn't have chosen for myself.

And as I watch my daughter embrace her "BIG BEING," I am filled with a profound sense of pride and joy. The garden I once nurtured so carefully is now flourishing, reaching towards the sun with its own unique beauty and strength. And I am grateful to have played a role in helping it grow.

As a mother, I understand the primal instinct to shield your child from every potential harm. Like many parents, I swore I would be there for my daughter, always ensuring her safety and well-being. But sometimes, good intentions can have unintended consequences. My fear of the unknown led me to overprotect my daughter, depriving her of the opportunity to learn and grow through independent experiences. That fear passed down from my childhood anxieties, unknowingly projecting a "smallness" message onto her. Today, she struggles with navigating uncharted territory, relying heavily on technology, and readily succumbing to panic when faced with unfamiliar situations.

This realization hit me like a wave: I had inadvertently clipped her wings, hindering her ability to spread them wide and soar. My desire to protect her had inadvertently held her back.

This experience isn't isolated. We see its echoes in the widespread negativity that permeates our online world. Social media platforms for connection and communication often become breeding grounds for hate, criticism, and judgment.

People hide behind anonymity, spewing venom and negativity towards others in a way they never would face-to-face. Their words, fueled by their own unresolved pain and insecurities, inflict wounds that can leave lasting scars on others.

Just like my overprotection, this online hate stems from fear. Fear of the unknown, fear of difference, fear of vulnerability. But instead of facing these fears head-on, they lash out, projecting their own smallness onto others in a desperate attempt to feel bigger and stronger. It's time we break this cycle. It's time to stop projecting our own fears and insecurities onto others. It's time to choose compassion over criticism, understanding over judgment. Imagine if we could use the power of online platforms for good instead of harm. Imagine using our words to lift others up, encourage, and empower instead of tearing down and destroying.

Let's break free from the shackles of fear and embrace the power of vulnerability. Let's choose to live BIG, not just for ourselves, but for the impact we can have on the world around us. Let's create a ripple effect of compassion and understanding, starting with ourselves and extending outward to build a world where everyone has the opportunity to shine their "BIG BEING" brightly.

We all carry within us a shadow self, a collection of negative emotions and unresolved issues that can manifest in unhealthy ways. Projecting our self-perceived smallness onto others through hate and criticism is a classic example of this shadow self in action.

Instead of celebrating the successes of others, we may feel envious and threatened, leading us to tear them down to feel big ourselves. This stems from a lack of self-awareness and a disconnect from our own unique purpose and potential.

But this doesn't have to be our reality. We can choose to unveil the shadow, confront its hold on us, and step into the light of our authentic selves.

Here are some questions to help you embark on this journey of self-discovery and shed the shackles of negativity:

1. How have you used your past to prevent a loved one from discovering their BIG?

Reflect on instances where you might have overprotected a loved one, shielding them from challenges and opportunities that could have helped them grow. Did your fear of their potential failure hold them back from experiencing their own "BIG BEING"?

2. How have you hated someone operating in their purpose?

Recall situations where you may have criticized or judged someone for pursuing their passions or achieving success. Did their accomplishments trigger feelings of inadequacy or self-doubt within you?

3. What do you believe is your purpose?

This is a crucial question that requires introspection and honest reflection. What drives you? What makes you feel passionate and fulfilled? What unique gifts and talents do you possess that can positively impact the world?

Answering these questions honestly and courageously is the first step towards embracing your "BIGNESS." By acknowledging how you have projected your smallness and identifying your own purpose, you can dismantle the negative habits that hold you back. Remember, you are not defined by your past mistakes or the shadow aspects of your personality. You have the power to rewrite your narrative and choose "BIGNESS."

Here are some additional ways to break free from the cycle of negativity:

• **Practice self-compassion:** Forgive yourself for past mistakes and acknowledge your challenges.

• **Focus on your strengths:** Identify and celebrate your unique talents and abilities.

• **Surround yourself with supportive people:** Build relationships with individuals who inspire and uplift you.

• **Challenge your limiting beliefs:** Identify the negative thoughts that hold you back and replace them with empowering affirmations.

• **Take action:** Start small and gradually move towards pursuing your goals and dreams.

The path to "BIGNESS" is not always easy, but it is undoubtedly rewarding. As you confront your shadow self and embrace your true potential, you will discover a world of possibilities waiting to be explored. So, take a deep breath, release the shackles of self-doubt, and step into the magnificent light of your "BIG BEING."

Chapter 12: See Yourself The Way God Sees You.

My journey towards being BIG is intricately woven with the threads of my faith. As a woman of Christian faith, I find my greatest strength, inspiration, and purpose in my relationship with Christ. He is the guiding light on my path, the unwavering rock beneath my feet as I navigate the often turbulent waters of life.

Every step I take towards embracing my "BIG BEING" is fueled by the scriptures that resonate within my soul. Verses like Ephesians 3:20 remind me that God's power working within me is limitless, capable of exceeding anything I could ever ask or imagine. And in Isaiah 43:19, I find comfort in knowing that I am a chosen vessel, fearfully and wonderfully made, with a purpose destined to unfold in His perfect timing.

My faith is not a mere accessory I wear on Sundays; it is the fabric of my being. It informs my choices, ignites my passions, and empowers me to dream big and reach for the stars. It teaches me to be compassionate, forgiving, and loving while also urging me to stand up for what is right and speak my truth with courage. Sharing my experience and faith with you is not about converting you or imposing my beliefs. It's about offering a glimpse into the source of my strength, the foundation upon which being BIG is built. It's about acknowledging the divine light within each of us, an excitement that yearns to shine brightly and make a difference in the world.

Just as Christ walked in BIG, loving unconditionally, healing the sick, and raising the dead, so too are we called to embrace our own "BIG BEING." We are all capable of extraordinary things, of leaving a positive mark on the world, and of reflecting the love and light of God in everything we do.

Belief: The Spark that Ignites Your Be BIG Journey

Belief, the cornerstone of the Be BIG Collective, is an invisible force that shapes our reality more than we realize. It is the fertile ground where our dreams take root and the fuel that propels us toward our goals.

At its core, belief is trust, faith, and confidence. It's a conviction in something, even when tangible evidence might be lacking. It's an unwavering certainty that whispers, "You can achieve this," even when the world seems to be shouting otherwise.

Right believing, however, takes this concept a step further. It implies trusting and having faith and aligning that faith with truth, aligning our beliefs with the reality we wish to manifest. Think of it like planting a seed. You can plant the seed, water it, and nurture it diligently, but without believing it will grow, the seed will likely remain dormant. Right believing acts like the sunlight that nourishes the root, fueling its growth and pushing it toward the surface.

But why is right believing so powerful? Here's why:

1. It shapes our perception: Our beliefs act as filters through which we experience the world. When we believe we are capable and worthy, we see opportunities where others see obstacles. We approach challenges with a confident optimism that can overcome seemingly insurmountable hurdles.

2. It attracts what we believe: The universe is a mirror, reflecting the energy we put out. When we believe in our potential, we radiate an aura of confidence and possibility that attracts positive experiences and opportunities. Conversely, negative beliefs can create self-fulfilling prophecies, blocking our progress and hindering our success.

3. It fuels our motivation: Belief is the fuel that propels us forward. It gives us the strength to persevere through setbacks and the courage to keep pushing even when doubts arise. Nothing can stop us when we truly believe in ourselves and our dreams.

4. It shapes our reality: Our beliefs don't just influence our perception; they also have the power to shape our reality. What we believe about ourselves and the world becomes our lived experience. Right believing empowers us to take control of our lives and manifest the reality we desire. So, how can we cultivate the right belief? Here are a few tips:

1. **Challenge limiting beliefs:** Identify and question negative beliefs that hold you back. Replace them with positive affirmations and counterevidence.

2. **Focus on gratitude:** Cultivate an attitude of gratitude for the good things in your life. This reinforces positive beliefs and shifts your focus towards abundance.

3. **Surround yourself with positive people:** Seek out individuals who believe in you and support your dreams. Their positivity can be contagious and help bolster your own belief system.

4. **Visualize success:** Spend time visualizing yourself achieving your goals. This helps program your mind for success and make your dreams more tangible.

5. **Act:** Belief is powerful, but it needs to be coupled with action. Take concrete steps towards your goals, even if they are small. Each step forward reinforces your belief and brings you closer to manifestation.

My faith didn't sprout overnight; it was nurtured from tender beginnings, watered by love, and shaped by the unwavering light of my grandmother, Nonnie. Even before I drew my first breath, Nonnie's spirit, steeped in faith, surrounded me. While she hadn't always walked the path of Christ, by the time I arrived, her dedication shone like a beacon, guiding me toward my own spiritual journey.

Nonnie wasn't just a believer but a pillar of our church, a "mother of the church" whose wisdom and faith resonated throughout the community. Every Saturday, she would transform our home into a haven of preparation for the Sabbath. The aroma of her delicious cooking filled the air, mingling with the steam rising from her crisp iron as she meticulously pressed her Sunday attire, complete with the white gloves that spoke of her reverence.

Nonnie's actions spoke louder than words. She didn't preach; she lived her faith. Her love for God radiated in her gentle touch, her warm smile, and the unwavering strength she displayed in the face of life's challenges. She taught me that faith wasn't just about attending church or reciting prayers; it was about weaving love and compassion into the fabric of every day.

Her quiet strength, unwavering dedication, and boundless love for God planted seeds of faith within me that continue to bloom today. Nonnie's legacy remains etched in my heart, a constant reminder that faith is a journey, not a destination, and that the greatest lessons are often learned not through words but through the powerful language of love and example. The Bible wasn't always an open book for me. It sat on the shelf, closed, its pages filled with words that seemed distant and cryptic. But over time, something shifted. Drawn by the warmth of stories and the whispered promises of a loving God, I began to delve deeper, turning the pages and letting the words wash over me.

It was a slow process, like a seed struggling to break through the hard soil. Each reading brought new insights, new challenges, and new understanding. I discovered stories of ordinary people facing extraordinary struggles, their flaws and doubts mirrored in my own. I witnessed their triumphs and learned from their failures, finding solace in knowing that even the greatest heroes stumbled and faltered.

But the most profound revelation came from the words that spoke of God's love. It wasn't just a vague concept but a tangible force, a warm embrace that enveloped me in its tenderness. The Bible became a love letter from God, a roadmap for this journey called life.

It wasn't always easy to accept. My past experiences and ingrained beliefs created a thick layer of doubt and skepticism. But with each step of faith, each prayer whispered in the quiet of the night, the layers began to peel away. The words on the page started to resonate with my soul, painting a picture of a God who saw me, loved me, and had a plan for my life. This journey of faith continues. There are still days when doubts creep in, and the path seems uncertain. But now, I have a compass – the words of the Bible, a love letter from God that reminds me of who I am and who He created me to be. It's a constant source of strength and inspiration, guiding me through the storms and illuminating the path toward my "BIG BEING."

Imagine, for a moment, wearing a garment woven from pure light. It drapes across your shoulders, not hiding your flaws but illuminating them from within. This is how God sees you – not with the flawed vision of man, but with a gaze that pierces through the surface to reveal the magnificent essence He created.

This vision goes beyond physical beauty; it delves into the depths of your soul, recognizing the inherent greatness that lies dormant within. Perhaps you have been mocked for your appearance, your words, or your unique spirit. But remember, those who judge by outward appearances are blind to the masterpiece that lies within.

To deny the greatness within yourself is to deny the very essence of God. He breathed life into you, infusing you with a touch of His own divinity. To see yourself as He sees you is to embrace that spiritual light, to recognize the potential for "BIG BEING" that lies dormant within.

It's not just about feeling good about yourself; it's about unleashing the power that resides within your soul. When you see yourself through God's eyes, you are freed from self-doubt, empowered to take risks, and driven to fulfill your unique purpose. You become a beacon of light, radiating love and compassion and inspiring others to discover their own "BIG."

Whether you believe in God or follow another spiritual path, the principle remains the same. Get still, quiet your mind, and contemplate how you see yourself. Is it aligned with the vision of your creator, the source of your being, or is it filtered through the lens of societal expectations and self-doubt?

Imagine yourself standing on a mountaintop, bathed in the golden rays of the rising sun. Your shadow stretches out before you, long and dark, but it cannot extinguish the brilliance radiating from within. This is the essence of seeing yourself as God sees you – recognizing the immense light that shines from the depths of your being, a light capable of illuminating the world around you.

In Matthew 5:14, Jesus proclaims, "You are the light of the world. A city set on a hill cannot be hidden." These words are not a mere compliment but a declaration of your inherent "BIG BEING." You are not a flickering candle in the darkness; you are a radiant fire, a beacon of hope and inspiration for those around you.

Just as the sun doesn't need validation from the moon to shine, your light doesn't require external recognition to be real. It exists because God breathed life into you, filling you with the blissful light that illuminates your soul.

But how do we access this inner light and let it shine brightly? Here are three steps to help you on your journey:

1. Shift your focus from self-criticism to self-compassion. We are often our own harshest critics, dwelling on our flaws and shortcomings. This negativity obscures our inner light and prevents us from embracing our "BIG;" instead of focusing on what we perceive as imperfections, we practice self-compassion. Acknowledge your weaknesses, but don't let them define you. Remember, you are still a work in progress, and your journey is what makes you unique.

2. Connect with your purpose. Just as the sun aims to illuminate the world, you, too, have a unique purpose in life. Discovering this purpose is crucial to unlocking your inner light. Reflect on your passions, talents, and values. What gifts do you possess that can positively impact the world? What problems are you drawn to solving? By aligning yourself with your purpose, you tap into a source of energy and motivation that will propel you forward on your Be BIG journey.

3. Share your light with the world. Don't let your light remain hidden. The world needs your unique brilliance, your compassion, and your courage. Find opportunities to express yourself and use your gifts and talents to uplift and inspire those around you. Whether volunteering your skills, starting a creative project, or simply sharing a kind word, every act of generosity and love helps illuminate the world.

Remember, seeing yourself as God sees you is not about ego or self-importance. It's about recognizing the holy gleam within you, the "BIG" that allows you to be a force for good in the world. Let your light shine not to gain attention but to illuminate the path for others and show them the "BIGNESS" that resides within themselves.

The scriptures I shared hold profound truths about your "BEING BIG," truths that can transform our lives when we truly grasp their meaning.

Fearfully and wonderfully made: This phrase from Psalm 139 captures the essence of our inherent "BIG." We are not random occurrences; we are intricately designed by a caring God who has placed a distinctive essence of divinity within every individual. This awe-inspiring creation process should fill us with reverence for ourselves and each other. It shatters the illusion of invisibility and reminds us that we are worthy of being seen, heard, and loved.

Thoughts of peace and not evil: Jeremiah 29:11 offers another powerful affirmation of our "BIG BEING." It assures us that God's plans for us are filled with "peace and hope," not despair. Just as we often think about those we love, picturing their happiness and success, so does God envision a bright future for us. This knowledge should dispel any doubts about our worth and purpose. If God has invested so much love and thought into our lives, how dare we not embrace our "BIG" and live to our full potential?

From thoughts to reality: Our thoughts have immense power. When we dwell on negativity, we attract negativity into our lives. Conversely, focusing on positive thoughts and affirmations paves the way for positive experiences. Knowing that God's thoughts about us are positive and hopeful empowers us to align our thoughts with this vision. By believing in the "BIG" God sees within us, we pave the way for its manifestation in our lives.

Here are some ways to integrate these powerful truths into your journey towards "BIG":

1. Reflect on your unique creation: Take time to ponder the wonder of your existence. Meditate on Psalm 139 and visualize the care and precision you were created with. This practice will cultivate a deep appreciation for your inherent "BIG."

2. **Align your thoughts with God's thoughts:** Repeat affirmations like "I am fearfully and wonderfully made" and "God has a plan of peace and hope for my life." This will help you internalize these truths and attract positive experiences into your reality.

3. **Take action toward your dreams:** Don't let the knowledge of God's love and hope for your life remain passive. Translate it into concrete actions and steps that move you closer to your goals and aspirations.

4. **Share your "BIG" with the world:** Let the light of God's love and your own unique "BIG" shine through you. Share your talents, gifts, and compassion with others, inspiring them to embrace their own potential.

Embracing the truths revealed in these scriptures leads you to self-discovery and transformation. You move from feeling invisible to recognizing your inherent "BIG."

You release self-doubt and embrace the future filled with "peace and hope" that God has envisioned for you. This is the essence of Be BIG – living a life aligned with your true potential, leaving a positive mark on the world, and illuminating the path for others to do the same.

Remember, you are not alone on this journey. God is with you every step of the way, cheering you on and guiding you toward your "Bigness." So, take a deep breath, step into your power, and Be BIG. The world needs the light that only you can bring.

Chapter 13: Decide to see yourself BIG!

Now that you know and understand how the Creator sees you, you must decide to see yourself - the way God sees you. Understanding how the Creator perceives you is a powerful revelation, but it's only the first step on a transformative journey. The next crucial decision lies in aligning your own vision with this divine perspective. This choice to see yourself the way God sees you is not passive acceptance; it's an active, conscious decision that ripples through every aspect of your life.

Decisions are potent forces, propelling us forward and shaping our reality. Look back at your life and see the tapestry woven from your choices. The path you walk, the education you pursued, the career you built - all stemmed from past decisions, big and small: each one, a thread in the intricate design of your present.

Please think of the decision to pursue education, whether it was entering school for the first time or returning later in life. It wasn't simply about acquiring knowledge; it was a declaration of your potential, a commitment to open doors and expand your horizons. This decision, fueled by ambition and hope, contributed to the abundance of career options you now hold.

Similarly, choosing to start a new business wasn't just about chasing a venture; it was an act of self-belief, a testament to your inner strength and resilience. This decision, born from a desire to carve your own path and trust your own vision, builds your confidence and propels you toward achieving your long-term goals.

And perhaps the most profound decision of all, the choice to love and be loved, manifests in the creation of a family. This decision, rooted in a yearning for connection and belonging, fosters a haven of shared experiences and unconditional support. It allows you to give and receive love, enriching your life in ways that transcend mere individual pursuits.

Every decision, every choice you make, is a brushstroke on the canvas of your life. But when you align your choices with the Creator's vision, you transform your journey into a masterpiece. Seeing yourself through divine eyes empowers you to make choices that resonate with your deepest purpose, leading you closer to a life filled with meaning, fulfillment, and the profound love that only comes from aligning your will with the divine.

The dust has settled, the choices made, and the consequences, good, bad, and everything in between, have become the stepping stones on your path. You've recognized the power of decisions, those potent conclusions reached after careful consideration. Now, it's time to delve deeper to mine the gems of wisdom hidden within the echoes of your past. Grab your journal, that trusted confidant, or a simple sheet of paper and a pen. Let them become your excavation tools, unearthing the buried treasures of your past decisions. Write them down, these crossroads of your life, each a turning point, a whisper in the wind shaping your journey. Don't shy away from the spectrum of outcomes, the successes that brought sunshine, and the stumbles that left you in the dust. Embrace the good, the bad, the ugly, and even the indifferent, for each one holds a lesson, a whispered truth waiting to be heard.

But our reflection doesn't end with mere recounting. Analyze, dissect, and interrogate. What were the takeaways from each decision, the hidden gems of wisdom that crystallized in the aftermath? Did you learn about your strengths, weaknesses, fears, and desires? Did you discover new paths you never knew existed, or did you reaffirm the ones you were already on? Let the epiphanies bloom. Let the 'aha!' moments light up the corners of your mind, for these are the maps to your future self.

Now, close your eyes with your journal overflowing with insights and your heart brimming with newfound awareness. Take a deep, cleansing breath, letting go of the past and welcoming the possibilities of the present. Inhale the vastness of the universe, the unbridled potential that resides within you. Feel your feet rooted in the earth, your connection to the very fabric of existence. And then, with a gentle exhale, rise. Rise above the limitations of your past, above the whispers of doubt, and step into your full potential.

This is Being BIG. It's not about physical stature or fleeting fame; it's about embodying the magnitude of your spirit, the boundless possibilities that lie dormant within. It's about recognizing your interconnectedness with everything around you and acting with purpose, compassion, and a deep understanding of your place in the grand scheme of things.

As you embark on this introspective journey, remember that my "BIG" is not yours to claim, nor is it meant to be a rigid blueprint. Instead, let's consider it a motivation, an invitation to kindle your vision. So, once more, close your eyes, reconnect with the echoes of your past, and inquire within yourself:

What does my BIG look like?

Is it a canvas exploding with vibrant colors, a symphony of your passions and dreams? Or is it a serene landscape bathed in the quiet confidence of inner peace? Perhaps it's a towering mountain, a testament to your resilience and unwavering determination. Don't be afraid to get specific! Does your BIG involve building a sustainable community garden, composing soul-stirring music, or championing a cause close to your heart? Paint your vision in vivid detail, and let it shimmer with the light of your desires.

What does my BIG feel like?

Is it the exhilarating rush of wind whipping through your hair as you stand atop that mountain? Or the warm, fuzzy embrace of belonging in a community you helped create? Maybe it's the quiet hum of satisfaction as you pour your heart into your art, knowing you've touched someone's soul. Allow yourself to feel the emotional resonance of your BIG, the joy, the excitement, and the fearlessness that fuels your spirit.

Does my BIG need to be tweaked? If so, how?

Your vision is a living, breathing entity, ever-evolving with your experiences and insights. Be honest with yourself. Does your BIG feel slightly out of reach? Does it need a touch of pragmatism to bridge the gap between dream and reality? Perhaps it needs a sprinkle of courage to push you past your comfort zone. Or maybe it simply needs a moment of quiet contemplation, a chance to refine its edges and let its true essence shine through.

Finally, decide to see yourself BIG.

This is the culminating act, the moment you step into the canvas of your creation. Imagine yourself standing tall, your shoulders broad, your eyes filled with the unwavering fire of your BIG. Feel the power coursing through you, the confidence that comes from knowing your purpose and embracing your potential. You are the brushstroke that paints the world with your unique brilliance.

A Journey of Positive Affirmations

For decades, you've sown the seeds of positivity through daily affirmations, whispered into the vastness of the universe. This unwavering commitment to the power of words speaks volumes about your dedication to shaping your destiny. You understand that words, like ripples in a pond, carry far-reaching consequences, capable of manifesting the life you desire or the one you fear.

Your belief finds its roots in the wisdom of Proverbs 18:21, a verse that echoes through the ages: "Death and life are in the power of the tongue: and they that love it shall eat the fruit thereof." This scripture serves as your guiding light, reminding you that your voice and words hold the power to sculpt your reality. Each positive affirmation is a brushstroke on the canvas of your life, painting a vibrant future brimming with joy, success, and fulfillment.

But the power of affirmations lies not just in their outward manifestation. They also weave their magic within you, shaping your mindset and fostering a sense of unwavering self-belief. As you speak words of affirmation, you plant seeds of hope and optimism in the garden of your mind. You water them with trust and nourish them with unwavering conviction. With each repetition, these seeds grow stronger, pushing through the doubts and anxieties that may arise.

My tongue, once a portal of anxieties, has been reforged in the fires of positivity. For years, I've wielded it as a sculptor, carving out the life I desire, word by word. "Broke" is a word I haven't spoken in ages, a rusty relic of a past self I've outgrown. It feels almost alien, like a language forgotten in a forgotten dream.

This transformation isn't just a matter of habit; it's an act of faith, a testament to my communion with the divine. My affirmations are prayers whispered into the cosmos, verses plucked from the pages of scripture, and woven into the tapestry of my being. "Fearfully and wonderfully made," I declare, feeling the echo of God's artistry in every fiber of my existence. "Triumphant," I proclaim, standing tall amidst the memories of past challenges, my spirit unbowed.

These affirmations aren't mere wishes cast upon the wind; they are seeds sown in the fertile soil of my belief. I tend them with unwavering conviction, watering them with the rain of patience and nurturing them with the sunshine of gratitude. Each repetition is a brushstroke on the canvas of my life, painting a vibrant future where "prosperity" dances with "insight" and "BIG" stands as my middle name.

Ever since I was a child, my mouth was a runaway train of declarations. "Watch me; one day, I'll have my own show," I'd announce to anyone within earshot, the air vibrating with the conviction of an individual with a microphone for a tongue. College wasn't much different. My dorm room walls echoed the spoken dreams, each word like a flashing neon sign, sounding off my audacious ambition: "Talk show host extraordinaire, coming soon!"

But the fire dimmed between late-night Chicken King, Busy-Bee's and Burger King runs, and life circumstances. The affirmations became whispers tucked away in the dusty corners of my mind. That's when my best friend reminded me of the dream. I had been shouting from the mountaintop but had been allowed to fade against life's challenges.

"What happened to your talk show? I thought I was supposed to be the Gayle to your Oprah?"

Her playful reminder was a sword of truth, a jolt of electricity to my dormant spirit. Suddenly, the dusty affirmations awakened anew, their edges sharpened by accountability and love. The universe, it seemed, was waiting for me to stop daydreaming and start doing.

Then, fate intervened in the form of a chance encounter. A woman who would become my rock-solid publicist and dearest friend saw the glow in my eyes and heard the echo of my unfulfilled promise.

"Public access television," she said, her voice laced with the magic of possibility. "Create your own show, girl. You've got the voice, the vision, the whole dang shebang."

And just like that, in 2014, Access 21 Charlotte welcomed a new face to its airwaves. Me. My dorm-room dreams morphed into a neon-lit reality, a microphone not just in my hand but in my soul. I had manifested a dream I had carried with me for years. I did what I said I would do, which became the catalyst for BIG, unbeknownst to me then.

My journey proves that words aren't just whispers in the wind; they're rockets aimed at the stars, carrying our dreams and the hopes and cheers of those who love us. So, speak your truth, my friend. Let your affirmations be battle cries, convictions, and anthems echoing through the universe. And when the doubts come creeping in, remember, you've got a whole cheering section behind you, ready to witness the magnificent manifestation of your words.

Take some time out for yourself today and write down ten positive affirmations, put them on post-it notes, and place them around your house. Next, I want you to do some mirror therapy and speak it out loud and BIG! You don't have to be BIG and loud daily, but I do want you to consider creating a lifestyle of speaking your positive affirmations daily. Use these ten blank spaces to begin.

1. _____
   _____

2. _____
   _____

3. _____
   _____

4. _____
   _____

5. _____
   _____

6. _____
   _____

7. _____
   _____

8. _____
   _____

9. _____
   _____

10. _____
    _____

I strongly suggest you get the Be BIG companion journal to assist you in your Be BIG journey. The journal provides additional sheets that can be printed as your new expanded view of yourself and helps you increase the positive things you have to say about yourself.

Chapter 14: Create A Like-Minded Village

The Be BIG journey isn't a solitary waltz in a spotlight; it's a vibrant, winding climb up a mountain, hand in hand with some fellow explorers and moments of solo reflection. While the view from the peak promises to be breathtaking, there will be stretches where the path feels lonely, the wind whistles doubt, and you might miss the familiar chatter of the valley below.

That's part of the tapestry, my friend. Choosing to change your life, to Be BIG, isn't just a personal shift; it can ruffle feathers in your circles. Some folks might not see the peak you glimpse through the clouds, clinging to the comfort of the ground below. This can be tough, demanding grace and patience with yourself and your loved ones.

Remember, your Be BIG journey doesn't mean abandoning your people; it's about inviting them along on a different path at their own pace. Share your vision and paint the picture of that breathtaking peak, but understand that some might need encouragement, gentle nudges, and maybe even a few "I told you so" when they finally join you at the top.

And for those lonely stretches? Embrace them. Savor the silence; use it to connect with your inner power and guide. Listen to God's whispers, let them carry your doubts away, and bring back wisdom on the wings of challenge. Trust that even in solitude, you're not truly alone. The spirit of Be BIG, the force of your own dreams, walks beside you every step of the way.

The Be BIG journey is like any epic adventure, with its exhilarating highs and treacherous lows. And the biggest challenge you'll encounter isn't a lurking beast or a perilous cliff face but the whisper of your own doubts. Brace yourself, for you'll face battles within the fortress of your mind, where negative thoughts stage their fiercest attacks.

They'll come disguised as whispers of "give up," seductive sirens luring you back to the comfort of the familiar. "This is too hard," they'll hiss. "Why push yourself? The old ways were easier." Remember, dear explorer; this struggle is a badge of honor, not a sign of weakness. You're attempting to climb a mountain most never dare dream of, and resistance is inevitable.

But here's the secret: your greatest enemy also holds the key to your victory. Those negative thoughts are the echoes of old fears, shadows cast by past limitations. Acknowledge them, yes, but don't let them control you. Arm yourself with your affirmations, your battle-tested weapons of self-belief. Each positive thought is a sunlight missile, piercing the darkness and revealing the path ahead.

We are all captains of our own destinies, navigating the vast ocean of life not with sails and oars but with the powerful currents of our thoughts. When storm clouds of negativity steer our minds, the journey becomes bumpy, the shores we reach bleak and shadowed. But here's the hidden treasure: we hold the map to brighter horizons within us. Like a sun-kissed compass, the choice to think positively can guide us toward shores overflowing with joy and fulfillment.

In the daily squalls of doubt and worry, it's easy to forget that negativity isn't our only option. We can swap the storm clouds for gentle breezes of optimism, the thunderbolts of criticism for the warm rays of self-belief. Each negative thought we replace with a positive one is a gust of wind propelling us closer to our desired destination.

Imagine your mind as a fertile garden. Negative thoughts are noxious weeds, choking out the vibrant blooms of possibility. But through positivity, we become skilled gardeners, uprooting those weeds and replacing them with seeds of hope, confidence, and gratitude. With each positive thought we plant, we cultivate a garden of abundance, attracting opportunities and happiness like bees to sweet nectar.

Negativity, a shadow cast from the moment we take our first breath, clings to us like a familiar cloak. It whispers in our ears, a language we understand all too well. It's the path of least resistance, the well-worn groove in the record of our lives. But here's the paradox, the secret whisper in the wind: positivity isn't just some fluffy cloud; it's a potent force, a spiritual law as powerful as its shadow twin.

But unlike negativity, which slithers in effortlessly, positivity demands attention, a conscious choice to turn our gaze towards the sun. It's like learning a new language that requires intentional effort, practice, and perseverance. We might stumble and slip back into the familiar darkness, but each time we choose positivity, we chip away at the wall of negativity, letting the light seep through.

This BIG adventure journey demands that we remember our initial flicker, the fire that ignited this quest for growth. When doubts gnaw, when the familiar whispers of negativity lure us back, we must anchor ourselves in that initial decision. Though challenging, we must remind ourselves that the climb is worth the breathtaking view from the peak.

Think of it like cultivating a garden. Negativity is the weed that grows effortlessly, choking out the vibrant blooms of possibility. Positivity, on the other hand, is the delicate orchid, requiring careful nurturing and attention. But with each positive thought we plant, with each affirmation we water, we cultivate a garden of abundance, attracting opportunities and joy like bees to sweet nectar.

As you embark on this BIG adventure, prepare for a delicate dance: the dance of evolving friendships. Some companions on your current path might not understand or embrace your transformation. After all, if change is a mountain for you, it can be Everest for those who've known you playing small for years.

It's a bittersweet truth, a tug at the heartstrings. It's unfortunate, even sad that some people who call themselves friends might find comfort in your limitations. But here's the key: their comfort doesn't define your growth.

These departures aren't rejections; they're simply paths diverging. You're ascending, reaching for a wider horizon, and not everyone is equipped to climb that same mountain. Some will choose to stay at the base, clinging to the familiar landscape. And that's okay.

For those who choose to stay behind, don't harbor resentment. Celebrate the shared memories, the laughter, the moments that built you both. Let their comfort be a stepping stone, not a chain. And focus your energy on those who resonate with your "Magnitude," who cheer you on from the sidelines or climb alongside you, hand in hand.

The Be BIG journey may be an exhilarating ascent, but it's not always a shared climb. Companions you began with might falter on the terrain, their paths diverging from yours. This isn't a failure but an echo of Amos 3:3: "Can two walk together unless they are agreed?" This scripture asks us to navigate the delicate dance of connection as we ascend.

Fueled by the same fire as you, some companions will stride alongside, each step a shared victory. Others may find their pace faltering, burdened by different desires, or clinging to familiar valleys. It's not a judgment on them or you but a natural divergence on the map of life.

The challenge is embracing the ascent while cherishing the connections that made the journey possible. Don't abandon your friends for greener pastures, but acknowledge that your paths might fork. Share stories from the summit, but let their ears rest if the echoes don't resonate. Their climb might look different, winding through forests or scaling gentler slopes, but the destination – a life lived authentically – remains the same.

Perhaps, in time, their paths will rejoin yours, enriched by their unique journeys. Or maybe their love will be a silent anchor, cheering you on from the base as you reach new heights. Remember, the Be BIG journey isn't a solo trek but a tapestry woven with threads of connection, both close and distant. So, continue to climb, friend, with open eyes and a heart that treasures the bonds that carry you even as you soar toward the sun.

Some, like sturdy oaks, will grow alongside you, their roots intertwining with yours in a symphony of shared growth. They'll celebrate your triumphs, offer support in your stumbles, and cheer you on with every step. These are the gems, the kindred spirits who understand Be BIG's language and see the breathtaking view you glimpse through the clouds.

But others, like saplings in the shade, might struggle to reach for the sun. They might find your evolution unsettling, your newfound fire a scorching light in their familiar forest. This isn't a failure or a judgment. It's simply the nature of growth, a divergence of paths on the mountainside.

Change isn't a one-way street. Your Be BIG journey requires not just your own evolution but a willingness to understand and support the journeys of those around you. Share your vision and paint the picture of the peak, but don't force them to climb if their roots are tethered to the valley below.

Be prepared for misunderstandings, for whispers of judgment that might paint you as the "changed one." But don't let those whispers define you. You're not rejecting the past; you're embracing a brighter future. And if some find that light uncomfortable, their shadow, not yours, needs adjusting. The pressure to stay stagnant, the manipulation to remain the same, can be insidious. It's like a mossy hand reaching up from the valley, whispering of comfort and safety in the familiar darkness. But remember, comfort isn't growth. Safety isn't evolution. Being BIG is about stretching beyond your limits, reaching for that breathtaking peak, and inviting those who resonate with your spirit to join you.

Your Be BIG journey isn't just a physical ascent; it's a psychological expedition, traversing the treacherous valleys of your own doubts and the manipulative hands of those who fear change. As you rise, the whispers of negativity will grow louder, morphing into insidious tactics designed to keep you grounded, to muddy the path ahead.

The most potent weapon in this arsenal is manipulation. The pressure to stay the same, the subtle guilt trips, the veiled threats of lost connections – all designed to make you question your ascent, to paint the peak as a lonely precipice instead of a glorious vista. Remember, these tactics aren't personal attacks; they're simply the desperate grasping of those who find comfort in the familiar valley, even if it means stagnation.

Don't let the fear of loneliness trip you up. Your evolution might create temporary distance, but growth doesn't threaten true connections. Those meant to walk beside you on this Be BIG journey will find their way, their own paths converging with yours at unexpected turns. The loneliness you might feel is a temporary space, not a permanent fixture. Another tactic – exclusion. You might find yourself on the outside of invitations, ostracized by those who view your growth as a challenge to their own stasis. Remember, this isn't a reflection of your worth; it's a testament to the discomfort that change breeds in those who choose to remain small. Their attempts to pull you down are desperate to maintain their own equilibrium, even if it means sacrificing shared joy and potential.

But here's the truth: it's easier to pull you down than it is for them to climb up. While they might find solace in negativity and manipulation, your ascent illuminates the path toward a brighter future. Your refusal to remain stuck is a spark, a beacon that might eventually awaken their desire for growth.

Forget the myth of the friendship desert in later life. It's a dusty tale spun by doubt, painting a desolate landscape devoid of genuine connection. New faces aren't scarce realities; they're waiting to bloom under the same expansive sky you navigate. Making friends at any stage isn't as perilous as made to believe; it's a vibrant dance under a constellation of potential connections.

This Be BIG journey, your ascent to personal growth, isn't a solo expedition. It's enriched by the company of like-minded souls, individuals who resonate with your newfound fire. These connections aren't oases found after aimless wandering; they're seeds waiting to be sown in fertile ground. Yes, the landscape might look different. Gone are the days of instant friendships forged in schoolyards or water cooler chats. But the human desire for connection remains a constant reminder even in unfamiliar terrain. Explore new communities, delve into shared passions, and open your heart to life's serendipitous encounters.

Remember, your perception paints your reality. It will be difficult if you see difficulty in forging new friendships. But flip the script! Embrace the truth: making friends is as natural as breathing, as effortless as a smile. Choose optimism, let your spirit radiate the warmth of the welcoming sun, and watch how connections bloom around you like wildflowers after rain.

Have you ever heard the saying, "You attract what you are"? It's more than just a catchy line; it's the golden key to unlocking a world of friendship. Become the friend you seek. Exude the warmth, openness, and genuine zest for life you desire in your companions. Show up with a smile and a listening ear, ready to share your laughter and support, and watch how kindred spirits gravitate towards your radiant energy. Imagine, for a moment, your circle pulsating with the life force of fellow badasses. Secure, joyful, and supportive, these dream friends are not mythical creatures – they exist! But guess what? They're not hiding in some exclusive, secret Garden of Eden for Be BIG superstars. They're all around you, waiting to connect with someone who radiates the same vibrant energy.

And yes, there might be whispers, the hushed anxieties of the "smalls" who haven't embraced their own "Magnitude." Intimidation might cast a shadow on their faces, and insecurity might hold them back from reaching out. But remember, their limitations are not yours. Be the one who extends a hand, builds bridges instead of walls, and show them that the Be BIG community isn't a clique but a vibrant tapestry woven from threads of shared growth and mutual support.

So, cast aside the tired tale of the friendship desert. Step into the sunshine, smile wide and radiate the Big-hearted spirit within. Remember, you are a magnet for kindred spirits, waiting to connect with a fellow traveler on the path to joy and fulfillment. Be the friend you seek, embrace the ease of connection, and watch your circle blossom into a vibrant landscape of laughter, support, and shared victories. Because on the Be BIG journey, no one walks alone. We climb together, celebrate together, and build a community where every peak conquered is a shared triumph, and every hand outstretched is a bridge to a brighter future.

Embarking on the Be BIG journey is an exhilarating ascent, but it's not just a single, bold leap. It demands sustained strength – the strong commitment to hold onto your newfound magnitude amidst the inevitable doubts and the siren call of the familiar. This is where your tribe, your village of kindred spirits, becomes your compass and your shield.

Choosing to Be BIG is the exhilarating first step, but staying true to it, navigating the whispers of self-criticism, and the gravitational pull of comfort is where the real challenge lies. It's akin to building a heart – the initial spark is easy, but maintaining the dancing flames requires constant attention, the careful addition of fuel, and the unwavering support of those who understand the warmth it brings.

Your village, your tribe of like-minded individuals, fuels your fire. They share your vision, understand your struggles, and celebrate your victories. Their unwavering belief in your bigness becomes the wind at your back, propelling you forward when the path seems steep and the doubts grow loud. The whispers of doubt soften in their presence, replaced by the echoes of shared values and unwavering encouragement.

This journey isn't about reaching a single summit and planting your flag. It's a continuous climb, a constant growth process, fueled by the collective strength of your tribe and your own unwavering commitment to your authentic self. So, hold on tight to your bigness, lean on your village, and let their support guide you through the shadows and light your way towards a future brimming with potential, where your magnitude burns bright and illuminates the path for others to follow.

Your village is not just a collection of faces but a network of hands extended and hearts beating in sync with yours. They'll be the ones who remind you of your "Magnitude" when the shadows of self-doubt creep in. They'll be the ones who celebrate your victories, big and small, and offer a shoulder to lean on when the climb gets steep.

Think of it as a symphony. Everyone, playing their unique instrument, contributes to the grand melody of your Be BIG life. The supportive friend, the encouraging mentor, the joyful cheerleader, the silent observer who simply radiates belief in you – every role, every note, plays a part in the harmony of your journey.

You being "BIG" isn't just a solo performance; it's a ripple effect, a light that illuminates the path for others. Your courage to climb inspires those in your village, proclaiming the possibility of their ascent. Imagine the magic of a village where empowered and joyful women blaze their trails, shattering glass ceilings and igniting the flames of possibility in others. It's not just individual lives transformed; it is communities uplifted, generations empowered, and a world painted with the vibrant hues of authentic living. But maintaining your "BIG BEING" isn't about creating an exclusive club, a gated community for the enlightened few. It's about extending a hand, sharing the warmth of your bonfire, and inviting others to join the dance. Let your village be a safe haven, a space of unconditional support where vulnerability is met with understanding and courage is celebrated.

Everyone in your village will have their specific role in how they help you along the way. The different roles are supporter, encourager, prayer warrior, traveling buddy, resource locator, entertainment, listener, and mentor. Let me go into more detail about a few of the roles mentioned, such as the role of supporter. What are the characteristics of a supporter?

Supporter:

- **Beyond Belief:** They not only believe in you, but they actively champion your dreams. They're cheerleaders, yes, but also strategists, offering practical support like research, connections, or simply sounding boards.

- **Empathy Engine:** They're skilled at listening and feeling with you. They understand your frustrations, celebrate your joys, and offer a safe space for emotional vulnerability.

- **Silent Strength:** They don't need to be in the spotlight; their power lies in quiet consistency. They're the reliable presence, the dependable hand you can always count on, even when the rest of the world feels unsteady.

- **Positive Catalyst**: Their support isn't passive; it's proactive. They nudge you out of your comfort zone, challenge you to grow, and celebrate your progress, big or small.

Encourager:

- **Visionary:** They see your untapped potential, even when you can't. They paint a picture of your future success, reminding you of your brilliance and inspiring you to reach for the stars.

- **Resilience Coach:** They believe in the power of possibility, even amidst challenges. They help you reframe obstacles as opportunities, teaching you resilience and reminding you that setbacks are stepping stones.

- **Word Wizard:** Their words are magic spells, casting out doubt and replacing it with hope and confidence. They know how to use the right words at the right time, lifting your spirits and igniting your inner fire.

- **Contagious Spark:** Their excitement for life is infectious. Their laughter brightens your day, their optimism is a beam, and their energy motivates you to keep moving forward.

Prayer Warrior:

- **Spiritual Sentinel:** They stand in the gap between you and your challenges, wielding the power of prayer as a shield against negativity and doubt. They offer unwavering faith and a strong shoulder to lean on, even in the darkest times.

- **Discerning Intercessors:** They listen with their ears and hearts, intuitively understanding your needs and praying accordingly. They may not always share your specific goals, but their prayers are aligned with your highest good.

- **Fount of Hope:** They offer words of encouragement and comfort, reminding you that you are not alone. They share stories of answered prayers and miracles, fostering faith and hope during challenges.

- **Silent Vigil:** Their prayers are a constant undercurrent, supporting you even when you're unaware. They may not be physically present, but their spiritual connection offers strength and guidance on your journey.

Mentor:

- **Guiding Star:** They've walked the path before you and offer a clear map to navigate the challenges and opportunities ahead. They share their experience not to dictate but to illuminate the way.

- **Wisdom Wellspring:** They are a reservoir of knowledge and expertise, ready to answer your questions, offer solutions, and provide valuable insights. They challenge you to think critically and push your boundaries for growth.

- **Mirror of Truth:** They offer honest feedback delivered with kindness and compassion. They see your strengths and weaknesses and hold up a mirror that allows you to see yourself more clearly.

- **Unwavering Champion:** They believe in your ability to succeed, even when you doubt yourself. They push you to reach your full potential, celebrate your accomplishments, and offer a hand-up when you stumble.

Taking Action:

- **Map Your Village:** Identify the individuals in your life who embody these roles. Make a gratitude list acknowledging their support and expressing your appreciation.

- **Extend Your Circle:** Seek out connections with others who resonate with your Be BIG journey. Join communities, attend workshops, or reach out to mentors in your field.

- **Empower Others:** Pay it forward by becoming a supporter, encourager, or mentor for someone else on their own Be BIG journey.

Being big is an ever-evolving ecosystem. Roles and faces might shift, but the foundation of love, support, and shared growth remains constant. So, embrace the power of your village, cherish the individuals who play these vital roles, and together, ascend the Be BIG Mountain, reaching for a future as vibrant and joyful as the connections you share.

(1) List the friends or loved ones who you believe will and can evolve with you along with their roles.

(2) Identify what your role(s) is in the lives of your loved ones.

(3) List your fears around the possibility of leaving someone or some people behind.

What's the worst that could happen?

_____
_____
_____
_____
_____

What are the possibilities of creating a new village and community?

_____
_____
_____
_____
_____

The Be BIG experience is always better when shared, and I hope it is encouraging to know you don't have to do this alone and there will be people cheering you on.

Chapter 15: Determine To Stretch Yourself

We're not bound by strict obligations but rather empowered by choices. When it comes to being BIG, it's all about how you decide to approach things. It's not about mandates or rules—it's about the way you want to live and engage with the world. You have the liberty to choose how you'll tackle situations, the attitude you'll bring, and the impact you'll make.

It's your call on how you want to step up, take charge, and leave your mark, whether it's through kindness, resilience, passion, or determination. Being BIG is ultimately your personal decision on how you want to show up in your life and the lives of others.

I really want to encourage you to embrace the mindset of being BIG, just as you are. Sometimes, we don't realize our own strength or the impact we can have because we haven't acknowledged it yet. But guess what? You've always had that "Magnitude" within you; it just might not have been obvious. If you start believing in your own "BIGNESS," that's where the magic happens.

Your ability to be BIG isn't something for later—it's happening right now in every place you step foot. When you carry that belief with you, suddenly, everywhere you go becomes your opportunity to make a significant difference. It's about recognizing and owning that innate "Magnitude" within yourself, seeing the power you already possess, and letting it shine in every aspect of your life.

Breaking it down even further, being BIG means truly knowing yourself inside and out. It's about embracing your whole self—no apologies, no doubts, just complete acceptance that you are more than enough exactly as you are. Wherever you find yourself, there's no need for a different version of you because the you that exists is already fantastic.

Let me tell you why: it's because you've got everything you need within you. It's about capturing the essence of who you are—your character, your values, what you stand for. It's about understanding yourself deeply, being honest and open about it, and embracing that vulnerability because that's where your true strength lies. Being BIG is all about recognizing your worth, knowing your strengths, and standing tall in your authenticity. You're a complete package, just as you are.

Think of these descriptions as your personal essence, the core of who you are, no matter where you go. Whether it's the grand halls of the White House or a cozy housewarming, the idea is to carry yourself in a way that's authentically you. It's like packing your essence in your metaphorical suitcase—it goes wherever you go. Your essence is your true north, guiding how you behave, react, and engage in any situation. The goal? Be comfortable and genuine, whether in a high-stakes environment or just hanging out with friends. It's about bringing your unique flavor to every setting, owning it, and staying true to yourself, no matter the place or circumstance.

When To Be BIG:

Being BIG isn't limited by any personality type. Whether you're an introvert, extrovert, ambivert or anything in between, your "BIG BEING" shines through—it's just who you are—being BIG means breaking out of any box because there isn't one that can contain us. It's not just about me stepping out of the box; it's about us collectively being bigger than any confining boundaries. And here's the thing: there's no rulebook dictating how or when to be BIG.

We have the freedom to express ourselves however we feel, whenever it feels right—within sensible limits. That's the beauty of it. Labels or norms don't restrict our "Magnitude." It's about embracing the vastness of who we are together and making choices that resonate with our true selves. There's no one-size-fits-all here; it's about celebrating our diversity and letting that shine unapologetically. Being BIG isn't just about doing whatever I want—it comes with a sense of responsibility. People notice how I carry myself and the decisions I make, and that's a big responsibility. It's not a solo act; being BIG is about considering others, too. It's an unselfish choice to live authentically but with awareness of how my actions might impact those around me.

This means I've got to be smart about it. Using good judgment and understanding my audience—knowing what to say and how to behave—is crucial. It's about being perceptive and thoughtful, making sure my actions align with the situation and the people involved. Being BIG requires this balance of staying true to myself while being considerate and aware of how others perceive me. It's a fine line, but it's all about being genuine without causing unnecessary discomfort or misunderstanding.

One day, I had a conversation with one of my mentors about the whole idea of being BIG and how it applies to different situations. We talked about the importance of gathering enough information to make informed decisions and the need for self-discipline. But then, things took a turn when he suggested that we should tweak our personalities if we make others uncomfortable or offend them. I respectfully disagreed.

See, my mentor comes from a place of privilege—privileged, well-off, and a Caucasian male. I felt his privilege shaped his statement, and I found it a bit ignorant. I don't believe in altering who I am just to fit someone else's comfort zone, especially if it's based on their privilege and lack an understanding of different perspectives. It's not about causing discomfort intentionally, but it's also not my responsibility to change who I am fundamentally just because someone finds it challenging. There's a fine balance between being considerate and authentic. I believe authenticity should never be sacrificed for someone else's comfort, especially when it stems from a place of privilege.

What struck me was that he said this without realizing his audience—me, an African American woman and considered a minority in this country. My very existence, my melanin, precedes my personality and could cause discomfort for various reasons, a story on its own.

I mean, how could anyone propose changing something as intrinsic as skin color and/or personality just to make someone else comfortable? It's a reality I've grappled with my entire life. This conversation, happening years ago, came at a point when I was already navigating my journey toward Being BIG, although I hadn't put a name to it yet.

At that moment, I felt unseen, and I couldn't help but question the purpose of our dialogue. Was he subtly probing if something I said was offensive? It made me reassess my approach—maybe I had approached the conversation with new filters, but I also needed to set aside my righteous indignation to turn this moment into an opportunity for mutual growth. It was about finding that delicate balance between advocating for myself and extending an olive branch for understanding. There was a chance for both of us to learn, grow, and bridge the gap in our perspectives, and I wanted to seize that moment despite the discomfort it initially brought.

My "BIGNESS" extends beyond just myself; it's about considering others, too. So, I opened up to my mentor about how his words affected me deeply. As a black woman, I've grown up understanding the importance of reading the room, not just for social cues but for my safety, too. See, my melanin, as magical as it is, often gets misconstrued. It's like I've been handed this script where I must navigate spaces cautiously, ensuring I don't unsettle things.

I shared with him the weight of being a black woman—how my very presence can sometimes be misinterpreted as aggression and my existence deemed disruptive. It's as if my skin emits some harmful rays solely because of societal misconceptions. I wanted him to grasp the reality that my experience goes far beyond just a simple conversation. It's about a lifetime of adapting, being hyper-aware of how I'm perceived, and constantly maneuvering to ensure I don't disrupt the comfort of those who hold privilege.

Though I felt initially offended by the conversation, I left it feeling invigorated simply due to speaking my truth in moments, providing grace to my mentor, and allowing space for much-needed dialogue. Being BIG also means educating others along your journey. The only way for people to show up differently is to educate and show them how.

You must also be in spaces where people look different from you, experience life differently than you do, and think differently. People must be exposed to your BIG if things are going to change for the good of everyone. Privilege can be a dirty word, but it doesn't have to be anymore because you have decided to be BIG. That's your privilege, right there.

Chapter 16: Examples of When to Be Big

I made it clear to him that there's nothing inherently wrong with my personality. It's not on me to bear the responsibility for someone else's discomfort or their reasons for feeling easily offended. I firmly believe it's an individual's duty to examine why they might struggle with or judge another person's personality.

What struck me was the irony—he suggested altering personalities to avoid discomfort, yet here I was, experiencing that very discomfort because of who I am. It was a stark realization. My "BIGNESS" led me to choose education and grace over just walking away from someone I deeply respect and consider a mentor. I wanted to offer insight into a reality he might not have fully understood. It wasn't about blame or confrontation but about opening a dialogue, sharing experiences, and hopefully fostering a deeper understanding on both ends. Sometimes, educating and extending grace can be more impactful than walking away from ignorance.

He acknowledged that he hadn't seen things from my perspective before, and I genuinely believed him. It takes real courage to actively engage and spend quality time with people from diverse ethnic backgrounds beyond just theoretical knowledge of diversity and inclusion.

We discussed the complexity of being offensive and being offended. Offended means feeling hurt or irritated due to a perceived wrong or insult, while being offensive involves hurting someone's feelings. I shared my belief that most people don't intentionally set out to offend others. It's a delicate balance—sometimes, actions or words can cause unintended offense, and navigating these situations requires sensitivity and understanding. Recognizing that these nuances exist and that there's no malicious intent behind actions helps foster better communication and empathy among diverse groups.

It's crucial to introspect when we feel offended because, often, it's linked to something from our past that's been triggered. In more personal settings, where there's familiarity and understanding, feeling offended can indeed be genuine and valid. But in situations where we're not intimately connected, where we're strangers, acquaintances, or associates, it's worth doing an internal check.

I believe that in these settings, our feelings of offense might be less about the other person's actions and more about something within ourselves. It's like a reflex—sometimes, past experiences or sensitivities are nudged, and that's what offends. It's about acknowledging that sometimes, our reactions might be more about our baggage than someone else's intent. It's a call for self-reflection to understand why certain things affect us the way they do, especially in settings where there's less personal history or understanding between individuals.

In my view, feeling offended often ties back to our personal reasons rather than the actions of the person deemed offensive. I've encountered situations where I've been labeled as offensive or rude simply because I'm straightforward, honest, and direct— traits not welcomed in the South where I have chosen to reside. Yet, back home in Brooklyn, NY, my directness rarely raises any eyebrows.

The interesting twist comes when I must navigate the subtleties of language and communication. For instance, certain phrases like "precious," "honey," or "isn't that dear" don't quite align with my direct approach. I find myself being extra cautious not to interpret these expressions negatively, especially when my peers use them. It's a whole different style of communication—one that requires a different lens to understand.

Hearing someone say "precious" triggers thoughts of "ugly" because, in my experience, those indirect phrases often mask true intentions. It's a cultural nuance that I've learned to recognize and adapt to, understanding that these expressions might carry different meanings depending on the context and the person using them. It's all about deciphering these subtleties in communication to understand the intentions behind the words properly. It's important to be fair and acknowledge that these terms might not be offensive at all. The sentiment behind them could be entirely pure. My intention in pointing this out isn't to be divisive but rather to highlight how our upbringing shapes the filters through which we listen and interpret language.

In simpler terms, it's often just a matter of differences in communication styles. Yet, despite these differences being harmless, we tend to judge them, leading to offense. Building barriers based on these judgments is like creating a divide between people. Pastor Stephen Furtick of Elevation Church aptly describes this as "offense creating a fence," a spiritual divisiveness that separates us.

I believe these misunderstandings often stem from our inclination to view differences as negative rather than simply as differences. It's about recognizing and embracing these distinctions in communication without automatically attributing negative connotations. Understanding that our backgrounds shape how we perceive things is key to breaking down these fences and fostering more inclusive, understanding relationships.

I used that example to emphasize our role as BIG individuals in checking offense and examining our reactions. Understanding why something strikes us a certain way and how we choose to respond to it is crucial. I firmly believe that, at my core, my essence is genuine and adaptable to any room or situation—and that should be enough.

I made a significant decision a while back—I was done with the whole charade of molding myself into different versions just to fit in or be accepted. It was one of the driving forces behind my departure from Corporate America to become my own boss. Let me tell you, it was liberating! Corporate settings often left me feeling unaccepted, like I had to be someone I wasn't, and it left me unfulfilled daily. But that's a story for another time, one I touched on earlier.

Learning to code-switch became a way of life for me early on. I had different versions of myself for school, home, my mother, potential partners, church, various organizations—the list went on. It was exhausting, and I started feeling isolated and frustrated as time passed. My genuine self didn't seem to fit in many places, and that weighed on me. I began to question whose responsibility it was that I felt this way.

It took me a moment of reflection and introspection to realize that I held the reins here. I made a conscious decision to take ownership of my authenticity. Gradually, I've reduced my multiple representatives from seven or eight down to just two or three. It's a journey, not an instant transformation. Being BIG isn't about perfection; it's about progress.

I'm confidently navigating life with just a few versions of myself now because I'm still on this journey. I'm a work in progress, embracing every step of this evolving process. Celebrating milestones, learning from setbacks, and eagerly looking forward to continual growth and success in all aspects of my life.

When it comes to being BIG, there's never a wrong time because it's simply who you are. Here are a couple of examples illustrating where it's crucial to Be BIG:

Church: Being your authentic self in the church is incredibly important. Often, the church environment has been one where people felt they had to conform to fit in, from their appearance to their way of speaking and living. This pressure sometimes leads to judgments and discomfort. But imagine the impact when you show up just as you are—authentically. Your example can make a huge difference, making others feel more welcome and comfortable and shifting their perception of what it means to be genuine in that space.

Work: I've personally struggled with shrinking myself at work and not fully embracing my authentic self. It's an arena where imposter syndrome can rear its head, especially for women and even more so for women of color. Seeking support from a therapist to work through these feelings can be tremendously beneficial. Additionally, actively seeking out diversity and inclusion groups at work can provide a supportive community. These groups can empower you to show up authentically while still excelling and growing professionally. Joining these groups can make a significant difference in feeling accepted and valued in the workplace.

Romance: this hits close to home for me. For the longest time, I settled for less in the pursuit of someone's attention. I'd change who I was—liking what they liked, doing things I wasn't passionate about—to win their favor, hopefully. I'd often suppress my own truth, fearful of rejection or being left behind. I'd even alter my appearance to fit into what I thought might be appealing. At times, I found myself agreeing to things I wasn't ready for, making me uncomfortable just to please someone else.

If any of this sounds familiar to you, I want you to know you're not alone in this struggle. And most importantly, there's no judgment here. Society bombards women with a jumble of confusing, often superficial messages. One of the messages that really irks me is the idea of telling girls to be "nice" rather than "kind." It's an important distinction. I urge women, ladies, and girls to choose their own terminology and define it for themselves. The pressure to be "nice" instead of "kind" has led to so much pain and trauma for women. The MeToo Movement is a stark reminder of the consequences of these societal messages. I strongly believe that this "nice" narrative has roots in many of the issues that fueled that movement. It's time for us to empower ourselves with the language and values that truly resonate with who we are rather than conforming to outdated, damaging expectations.

The societal narrative ingrained in us often prioritizes superficial beauty over intellect, telling us that having a brain isn't the most appealing trait to a potential partner. This pressure pushes women to downplay their true selves, molding them into what they think will make their partners feel important and desirable. We shrink away from authenticity, believing this is the path to love and, someday, marriage. But the truth is, it's a disservice to everyone involved when we don't show up as our real selves. We may end up in relationships or marriages where our partners don't truly know who we are. Then, when our genuine selves start surfacing, confusion and conflicts arise. It highlights the vital necessity of Being BIG consistently, not just for us but for those we choose to love someday. I could dive into an exhaustive list of places where authenticity is a challenge, but I'll share just a few main areas here. I host Master Classes that delve deeper into these topics, offering comprehensive insights. I hope someday you'll join me in exploring these themes further and finding the courage to show up authentically in every aspect of your life.

Chapter 17: Who Is Big?

The core of who I am, the very essence of my existence, revolves around my deep connection to God. It's the anchor that shapes every thought and action in me. However, expressing this integral part of myself hasn't always been easy, especially in settings where it didn't feel safe or acceptable to share.

My faith isn't some neatly folded garment I wear to Sunday service and promptly tuck away until the next time propriety demands its display. It's not a performance, a costume donned for specific occasions. No, it's the very marrow of my bones, the silent thrumming of my heart, the invisible thread woven into the tapestry of my being. The sun casts long shadows over my choices, the compass that guides my every step and the wellspring from which I draw strength and solace.

Yet, expressing this core of me hasn't always been as natural as breathing. There have been spaces, sterile and cold, where my faith felt like a foreign language, and my proclamation of devotion met with raised eyebrows and polite smiles that never quite reached the eyes. In those places, I learned to cloak myself in a shroud of silence, to fold my wings and pretend I could fly no higher than the expectations set by others.

But the truth is, I can't not fly. My spirit yearns for the open sky, for the unfettered communion with the God that makes my soul sing. And so, I've learned to seek out pockets of sunshine, like-minded souls who understand the language of my heart, where my faith can unfurl like a vibrant banner, unashamed and unapologetic. In these spaces, I find not just acceptance but a chorus of kindred spirits, their voices weaving in harmony with mine, creating a symphony of shared belief that transcends the limitations of the mundane.

When I began my journey in the media world, I briefly worked with a publicist who suggested toning down my religious references. Their advice was rooted in a belief that openly expressing my faith might not align with the strategic path toward future success. But that guidance didn't sit well with me, and it certainly wasn't a viewpoint that stayed with me for long.

I struggled for years to find a genuine way to share my close relationship with God while navigating a society that occasionally gives the impression of being hostile to such openness. It was a fight that opposed my own effort to be true to myself while still fitting in with what appeared to be the accepted standard in some groups.

It felt like walking a tightrope strung between two sheer cliffs. On one side, the chasm of authenticity yawned, its depths beckoning with my faith's raw, unfiltered expression. On the other, the precipice of normalcy loomed, the ground below paved with unspoken expectations and societal norms that seemed to frown upon open displays of devotion.

For years, I teetered, my heart a pendulum swinging between the two. In some spaces, faith was a welcome guest, an invisible thread woven into the tapestry of conversation, acknowledged with knowing smiles and whispered prayers exchanged like secrets. But in others, it was a pariah, a foreign language met with raised eyebrows and polite but dismissive nods.

The pressure to conform was immense, and I learned to code-switch, to don a mask of nonchalance when the conversation strayed towards God. Once eager to sing His praises, my tongue grew hesitant, my words tripping over themselves in the face of perceived judgment.

But the silence gnawed at me. It was like trying to hold back the tide, a futile effort that left me drained and unfulfilled. My soul craved the open sky, the uninhibited expression of my love for God that made my spirit soar.

So, I started small. I found pockets of sunshine, like-minded souls who spoke the language of my heart. In their company, I could unfurl my faith like a vibrant banner, let the words cascade forth like a song, unburdened by fear or pretense. Scattered like hidden oases in the vast desert of societal expectations, these pockets became my havens, my sacred spaces where I could be unapologetically myself.

The journey wasn't always easy. There were still moments of doubt, whispers of insecurity that urged me to retreat into the shadows. But I grew stronger with each step, each shared prayer, and each conversation that bridged the gap between my inner world and the outer world. I learned to navigate the tightrope with extraordinary grace to hold onto my authenticity even in the face of perceived disapproval.

Slowly, the world around me started to shift. Conversations once stilted by awkward silences now flowed with genuine curiosity and respect. Friends who once seemed indifferent now sought my perspective, their own hearts opening to the possibility of faith lived openly and honestly.

My connection with God, however, is the most important aspect of who I am. It's not just a single aspect of my life; it's the core of who I am, the source of my power, and the direction I take in everything I do. Furthermore, even though the suggestion to tone it down may have originated from a strategic standpoint, in the end, it didn't fit with who I am at my core. That publicist and I didn't quite click, and it wasn't solely because of our differing perspectives. She reflected a common sentiment in her industry, advising me to dial down my religious references to navigate the professional landscape more easily. I get it; it's a viewpoint shared by many in that space, aiming for a strategic approach to success.

Yet, when it comes to my confidence and my sense of self, it's intimately tied to something far greater than myself. It's rooted in my unshakable connection with a higher power—a God who has been my constant companion through every twist and turn of my life's journey.

I couldn't imagine being less than honest about where my confidence and strength stem from. To hide or downplay the source of my resilience and fortitude would feel like denying a fundamental part of who I am. My confidence doesn't come solely from personal achievements or talents; it's deeply intertwined with the faith and trust I have in a God who has repeatedly shown up for me in remarkable ways.

Sure, it might not align with the strategic advice floating around in certain circles, but for me, authenticity trumps conformity. Being true to my faith isn't just a part of my identity—it's the core that sustains me, shapes my decisions, and gives meaning to every step I take. To hold back on acknowledging that would feel disingenuous, like denying a vital piece of my story and the force behind my very existence.

I'm grateful to God for being there for me when I felt unsure of myself. I went through tough times with teasing and not feeling accepted by others. I turned to God whenever I needed love and support to get through those days, and He never failed to provide it. I'm still grateful for what God has done for me now that those difficult days have stretched into months and years.

I immerse myself in His teachings every day via devotion and meditation, allowing them to seep into my spirit. It's not simply a facet of my existence; it's who I am in my heart. Assisting individuals who are seeking faith, interacting with other believers, and participating in my spiritual community are all aspects of this incredible trip I'm on.

I've learned that how I live out my faith might not be what everyone's into, and that's totally fine. Just as not everyone might be drawn to someone else's BIG, not everyone will connect with the message that defines my life—the message of my faith.

If you've let me share a moment of my story with you, I think there's a reason for it. It can be by faith, destiny, or just how things work out—I see it like God brought us together for a reason. He seems to have brought us together, allowing me to speak with you, and it might be a hint for you to share with me as well.

I've now come to peace with the idea that not everyone will share my beliefs or approach to living out my faith. That's the nature of life. You may also have to face the fact that not everyone will be drawn to your story or values. Sometimes, that's just how things work.

However, I believe it's an invitation—a permission slip, if you will—for people who are moved by my religion and my journey to consider and respect their own convictions. You must also acknowledge that not everyone will share your values or routes. However, for those, they find comfort, guidance, and the freedom to follow their own unique journeys.

When I confidently live out my BIG, it's like showing a sign to others looking for a place to belong—a welcoming community. It's like saying, "If you're like me and searching for a place to fit in, this is where you'll find support and acceptance."

I've learned that embracing my BIG isn't just for myself but also for those looking for someone they can relate to. It's about having a guiding light, that safe space for those on a similar quest to find their tribe.

And by embodying my BIG, I hope to offer that same permission and affirmation to those who might resonate with my journey. It's important to make a place where people feel good about themselves, where they can celebrate what makes them special and know that they're valuable just as they are. Retaining who we truly are helps us feel strong and inspire others to do the same.

Harriet Tubman's bravery in helping enslaved people find their way to freedom. Being willing to give her life so others could be free has always inspired me. Her bravery, sheer determination, and love for her people, motivating her to forge ahead despite the odds stacked against her, is an encouragement for me and countless others.

Then there's my mother, a living testament to perseverance. Her resilience, her refusal to give up even when the road got impossibly tough—her example has been my cornerstone, reminding me that giving up is never an option.

And Nonnie, oh, she embodied a deep, unshakable love for God. Her devotion and her wholehearted commitment to faith showed me the depth of what it means to love with every fiber of your being. Her unwavering connection with God taught me about devotion beyond measure.

Reflecting on these incredible individuals in my life, their bravery, resilience, and unwavering faith have become interwoven into the fabric of my journey. Their stories and virtues have shaped the way I navigate challenges, confront fears, and hold onto my faith in times of uncertainty. Their bravery inspires me to face my fears head-on, just as their perseverance fuels my determination to keep pushing forward, even when the path seems impassable. The depth of their faith has reminded me to hold onto my beliefs to trust in something bigger than myself.

So, I want to extend that same invitation to you—to think about those remarkable people in your life who've exemplified qualities you admire. It's about acknowledging how their stories and strengths have woven into the tapestry of your own journey, shaping who you are and how you face the world.

Embracing an abundance mindset is like opening the door to a world where there's space for everyone. We're all so wonderfully diverse, each carrying our unique narratives and living out our BIGs. Despite the differences in our paths, there is space for every one of us, and that is a great thing.

The abundant mindset emphasizes inclusion over exclusivity. It's about allowing each person to shine in their own special manner and carve out a niche for themselves without fear of rejection or judgment. It's simpler to be kind and accepting of other people when we embrace and value who we are.

It's about loving ourselves and others and being loved by something greater than ourselves. It is simpler to be receptive and welcoming to other people when we are filled with that inner confidence and love. That has a lot of power. I get that talking about personal things, especially faith, when you're a private person, can be tough. But by doing that, you're being strong and showing that your journey has been powerful and transformative. Sharing your story spreads a message of love and acceptance, which can really touch others going through their own journeys.

Take time out today or this week to discover your BIG WHO!

How has your "who" impacted your life?

How is your "who" directing your next steps and choices?

How do you choose to show gratitude to your "who"?

Chapter 18: What's Your BIG?

The concept of "big" is inherently subjective, a multifaceted term that weaves through the tapestry of individual experiences, aspirations, and perceptions. Its definition transcends a one-size-fits-all approach, morphing into a dynamic entity that adapts to the unique contours of each person's journey. At its core, "big" embodies the pursuit of substantial success, crafting a lasting impact in one's chosen sphere—professional, communal, or personal.

It is a multidimensional prism, capturing the essence of reaching milestones that hold personal significance, be they monumental achievements in a career, profound moments in one's personal life, or the realization of ambitious goals meticulously etched into the fabric of dreams.

The allure of "big" often carries with it the weight of accomplishment, the sweet taste of recognition, or the far-reaching tendrils of influence. The magnetic force pulls individuals towards their loftiest aspirations, beckoning them to surpass boundaries and transcend conventional limits.

"Big," in the realm of careers, may manifest as the pinnacle of professional achievement, a moment where tireless dedication culminates in a breakthrough that reverberates beyond individual realms. For others, the grandeur of "big" is sculpted within the intimate contours of personal life—a union, an accomplishment, or a revelation that leaves an indelible mark on the canvas of existence.

However, "big" unfolds as a journey, a series of interconnected chapters that collectively comprise the opus of a life well-lived. The audacious dream pursued, the relentless pursuit of excellence, and the courage to embrace challenges leading to transformative growth. The very essence of "big" resides in the ceaseless quest for self-improvement and the realization that each step, regardless of its perceived size, contributes to the overarching narrative of a purposeful existence.

So, "big" is not merely a destination but a dynamic process, an ongoing narrative that evolves as individuals navigate the intricate landscapes of their aspirations. It is the amalgamation of determination, resilience, and an unwavering commitment to charting a course that aligns with the core values and passions that define one's identity. So, the pursuit of "big" is a deeply personal odyssey. In this journey, the significance lies in the destination and the profound transformation that unfolds along the way.

My Be BIG:

I have a big personality that most folks don't see because I've become a serial entrepreneur. But those who've known me since my school days, my sorority sisters, family, my spouse, and friends I've made along the way know I'm super passionate. I care a whole lot about God, therapy, people, and animals.

Passion is my driving force, an unwavering flame that ignites at the mention of things closest to my heart.

God holds a profound place in my life; faith guides my steps and shapes my convictions. It's the cornerstone of my existence, lending me strength and purpose in every endeavor. And therapy? It's not just a profession; it's a testament to the belief in healing, growth, and the profound capacity for change within ourselves.

But it's not just about concepts—it's about people. People are my heartbeat; their stories, dreams, and struggles resonate deeply within me. Every connection forged feels like a thread woven into the tapestry of my life. And animals? Their innocence and unconditional love strike a chord in my soul; caring for them is both a joy and a responsibility I hold dear.

The depth of my personality might not always surface amidst the whirlwind of entrepreneurial pursuits. Still, behind the scenes, that fervor, that dedication to causes larger than life, is the driving force that fuels my journey. It's a tapestry woven with threads of passion for God, therapy, humanity, and the silent companionship of animals—a testament to the depth of my soul.

I adore books and all things academic—I'm a big fan of higher education and its vibes. I'm outspoken, love to laugh and be silly, sometimes awkward and geeky, and I'm a relaxed, laid-back person. I'm all about bling and stylish clothes, I've got a thing for shoes, and I'm obsessed with hair—both mine and others. I prefer to keep things minimal and believe in using what I have or tossing it out. My hubby might call me high maintenance, but that's just me!

I've got ADD, so if you want me to notice something, you might need to point it out. I once missed seeing my husband's new motorcycle in our garage for four days until he showed me! Can you believe it? That's just a quick glimpse of who I am.

You'll often find me speaking my mind and being outspoken about things I'm passionate about. But at the same time, I can't help but laugh and be silly—it's part of my nature. Sometimes, I embrace my awkward and geeky side; it's what makes me, ME. And relaxation? That's my mantra. I'm all about taking life in stride, being laid back, and just enjoying the moment.

Now, let's talk about fashion and style. I'm all about bling and stylish clothing and shoes. Oh, they're my weakness. There's something about a fabulous pair of shoes that can elevate any outfit. And hair? It's not just about my own; I'm low-key obsessed with how others style theirs. It's like an art form to me.

When it comes to belongings, I have this minimalistic approach. I firmly believe in using what I have or letting it go. Some might call it high maintenance, but to me, it's about appreciating quality over quantity and keeping things streamlined.

That's just a snippet of who I am—a blend of academic passion, outspokenness, style appreciation, and a dash of quirkiness that keeps things interesting.

But you know what? I love all of it, and I'm totally unapologetic about being me.

It took a while to get here, but it was worth every bit of the journey. I've learned to appreciate my own pace and timing—it's what makes my story unique. I don't compare my path to others, and that's helped me celebrate their successes while being thankful for my own journey.

I've realized I don't have to follow society's idea of success. I get to decide my path, and none of the usual labels—age, race, gender, appearance, or past—define how I should go about it. Every new day is a chance to be true to myself and embrace my uniqueness.

Your Be BIG:

Authenticity is like a superpower; it's what makes each of us unique and compelling in our own way. Trying to emulate others instead of embracing our genuine selves is like dimming our own light.

Look at these incredible figures mentioned: Oprah, Les Brown, TD Jakes, and Tony Robbins. Each of them shines because they've tapped into their authenticity: Oprah's empathy and connection ability, Les Brown's powerful storytelling, T.D. Jake's inspirational wisdom and Tony Robbins' boundless energy have all harnessed their true essence to become influential leaders.

When we're true to ourselves, something magical happens. We connect more deeply with others because authenticity breeds trust and relatability. People are drawn to authenticity because it's real and genuine. It creates a sense of comfort and openness that allows others to be themselves, too.

We can learn from these remarkable leaders and adapt certain qualities or skills, but the key is to integrate those lessons into our own unique selves. Our special blend of experiences, perspectives, and personality traits is what sets us apart and enables us to make our own mark in the world.

Remembering that authenticity is our greatest asset encourages us to embrace our quirks, flaws, strengths, and passions. It liberates us from the pressure of trying to fit into someone else's mold and allows us to unleash our full potential.

We cling to the seductive notion of the "whole plan," a detailed life itinerary. We yearn for a crystal-clear roadmap to our dreams, a GPS for the soul that reveals every twist and turn, leading us effortlessly to the triumphant finish line that shimmers in our imagination.

Forget the pressure of a predetermined path. Embrace the organic exploration, the thrill of discovery, and the satisfaction of navigating life's unexpected turns. Let your journey be a canvas where each moment adds a brushstroke, painting your own unique masterpiece. Ditch the map, my friend, and gather the mosaic of your heart. The world is your oyster, and every experience is a pearl waiting to be found.

But the truth is, life rarely operates on such a tidy blueprint. The "whole plan" is less like a map and more like a mosaic. We gather the pieces, vibrant and diverse, each holding a fragment of the bigger picture. Some pieces fit neatly, others require chipping and shaping to find their place. And the beauty lies in the process itself, not just the final image.

Imagine if we saw the entire mosaic upfront, the vast expanse of tiles stretching before us. The sheer magnitude might cripple us, the fear of the unknown a paralyzing force. We might freeze, overwhelmed by the journey ahead, unable to even pick up the first tile.

But the magic happens in incremental steps. Each piece we place, each challenge we overcome, adds a splash of color and a burst of texture to the growing mosaic. The small victories, unexpected detours, and moments of doubt and perseverance all weave a narrative far richer than any pre-written script.

It's like climbing a mountain. We don't see the summit from the base, shrouded in mist and hidden by the climb itself. But we take each step, trusting the path beneath our feet, marveling at the changing vistas with each turn. The exhilaration of reaching a plateau, the thrill of conquering a challenging climb - these are the rewards that fuel our journey, not just the distant peak.

So, let go of the need for the "whole plan." Embrace the mystery, the unfolding story. Focus on the piece in your hand, the step in front of you. Trust that every experience, every encounter, every obstacle is a brushstroke on your grand mosaic. Believe in the power of the small steps, the quiet victories, the unexpected turns that lead you closer to your dream.

And remember, the most beautiful mosaics are often the ones built with imperfect pieces, each crack and imperfection telling a story of resilience and growth. So, embrace the journey, celebrate the process, and trust that your dream, like a magnificent mosaic, will come together, one vibrant tile at a time.

Set aside some time to figure this out—it's worth the extra moments. You're going to answer some questions about who you are right now, not who you want to become. The aim is to discover your current BIG, acknowledging that you're already enough as you are today.

***

Who are you?

Where were you born?

What's your ethnicity?

___

What's your gender?

___

How much do you weigh?

_____

_____

_____

_____

_____

_____

_____

What's your shape and shoe size?

_____

_____

_____

_____

_____

_____

_____

_____

_____

What's your dress/pant size?

___

What's your personal style? Are you chic and simple or flashy and snazzy?

___

What's your hair color, length, and texture?

_____
_____
_____
_____
_____
_____
_____
_____

What's your education?

_____
_____
_____
_____
_____
_____
_____
_____

What is your current career?

_____
_____
_____
_____
_____
_____
_____
_____
_____

What's your personality type? (Please refer to Myer-Briggs free personality assessment) According to a large study published in Nature Human Behavior, there are four main personality types: average, reserved, self-centered, and role model.

_____
_____
_____
_____
_____
_____
_____
_____
_____

Are you a private or an open book?

_____
_____
_____
_____
_____
_____
_____
_____
_____

What are your hobbies?

_____
_____
_____
_____
_____
_____
_____
_____
_____
_____

What foods do you enjoy?

What people are you attracted to?

***

The beauty of character development lies in its organic nature. This worksheet acts as a launchpad, propelling you into the inner world of your creation. It provides a compass, not a rigid map, allowing you to navigate your character's depths while leaving room for unexpected twists and turns.

Remember, your character is a living, breathing entity, evolving with each chapter, each encounter, each brush with adversity. Their initial traits, motivations, and challenges are stepping stones, not constraints. Let them surprise you with hidden strengths, unexpected vulnerabilities, and moments of growth that defy your original plan.

Embrace the contradictions, the internal struggles, and the gray areas that make your character a tapestry of emotions and experiences. Allow them to be shaped by the world around them, react impulsively, make mistakes, and learn from them.

As you write, listen to their inner voice. Let their fears and desires whisper through the narrative. Give them agency, letting them make choices that may diverge from your initial vision. This is where the magic happens, where your character truly comes alive, exceeding the confines of the worksheet and stepping onto the stage of your story.

So, dive into the depths of your character's psyche with this foundation, but do so with an open mind and a playful spirit. Be ready to be surprised, challenged, and ultimately rewarded by their unfolding journey. Remember, the most compelling characters are the ones who surprise us, not just the reader, but even ourselves.

And above all, have fun! Enjoy discovering who your character is, one chapter, one heartbeat, one unexpected turn at a time.

Chapter 19: Conclusion

We've covered the why, what, who, when, where, and how of Being BIG, offering chances for you to reflect and process along the way. For those who got the companion journal, it's an added opportunity to delve deeper into your thoughts and realizations.

Now, you might be wondering, "How will I know if I'm transformed or on the path to Being BIG?" Firstly, give yourself time and grace in this journey. Just by purchasing this book and taking this step, you're already on the right track toward evolving into your BIG self. Transformation comes with signs, but it requires mindfulness and being present in your now.

Secondly, breathe. This is not a race to the finish line nor a quest for immediate perfection. Simply by taking this step, purchasing this book, and opening your heart to the possibility of growth, you've already planted the seeds of transformation.

Remember, a mighty oak doesn't sprout overnight. It takes time, patience, and the gentle nourishment of rain and sun.

But transformation, like a bud pushing its way through the earth, will leave its mark. Here are some whispers of its presence, signs that you're on the right path:

Inner shifts:

- **A newfound sense of clarity:** You see the world with fresh eyes, your values and priorities aligning with your authentic self.

- **Increased compassion:** You find yourself drawn to others, offering kindness and understanding with an open heart.

- **A surge of courage:** You step outside your comfort zone, embracing challenges with newfound confidence.

- **The quiet hum of peace:** Even amidst life's storms, a sense of inner calm washes over you, a knowing that you are on the right path.

Outer ripples:

- **Synchronicity and serendipity:** Opportunities seem to unfold effortlessly, doors opening as you approach them.

- **Healthy relationships:** You attract and nurture connections with people who uplift and inspire you.

- **Meaningful work:** You find yourself drawn to pursuits that ignite your passion and contribute to something bigger than yourself.

- **A sense of purpose:** You understand your unique place in the world and your contribution to the grand tapestry of life.

Remember, these are just whispers, not a rigid checklist. Every journey is unique, and the signs of transformation will manifest in ways that are personal to you. Be present, be mindful, and pay attention to the subtle shifts within and around you. Trust that you are on the path, and celebrate each step, each ripple of change, as a testament to your ongoing evolution.

And remember, your companion journal is not just a record of your journey. It's a map you co-create. Fill its pages with your thoughts, your fears, and your breakthroughs.

Stay aware of the present moment, as it holds the clues to your evolution. You might notice subtle shifts in how you react to situations, perhaps feeling more authentic or confident in expressing yourself. There might be a growing sense of alignment between your actions and your true values.

These signs might be small, but they're indicators that you're on your way to embracing your "BIGNESS." Keep an eye out for these changes—they're proof of your ongoing transformation.

Let's delve deeper into the subtle whispers of transformation that guide us on the path to embracing our "BIGNESS." Here are some ways to stay present and tune into these clues:

Inward echoes:

- **Shifting reactions:** Notice how you respond to situations, challenges, and even everyday interactions. Do you feel more empowered to express your true self, even when it differs from expectations? Do you find yourself choosing grace over anger, understanding over judgment? These are subtle but powerful signs of your inner compass recalibrating.

- **Values whisper:** Pay attention to what resonates with you. Does your heart leap with joy at the thought of pursuing a passion project, even if it seems risky? Do you find yourself drawn to causes that align with your core beliefs? These are whispers of your authentic values guiding you toward a life of meaning and purpose.

- **Confidence ripples:** Observe the quiet hum of confidence within you. Do you feel more comfortable speaking your truth, setting boundaries, and taking ownership of your decisions? This newfound self-assurance is a testament to your growing inner strength and the blossoming of your BIG self.

Outer reflections:

- **Synchronicity's dance:** Notice how seemingly coincidental encounters or unexpected opportunities seem to pave your way. Doors open as you approach, and connections form with like-minded souls who inspire and support your journey. These are the universe's gentle nudges, guiding you toward your "BIGNESS."

- **Relationships that bloom:** Reflect on the connections you cultivate. Are you drawn to individuals who challenge you to grow, who celebrate your victories, and who hold a mirror to your authentic self? These are the reflections of your evolving "BIGNESS," the nourishing soil in which you flourish.

- **Purpose's calling:** Listen to the whispers of your soul. Do you feel a pull towards a specific path, a cause that ignites your passion, or a contribution you yearn to make? This is the echo of your unique purpose, beckoning you to step into your "BIGNESS" and make a difference.

- **Alignment's melody:** Observe how your actions align with your desires. Do you find yourself making choices that resonate with your deepest values, even if they seem unconventional? This is the harmony of your BIG self coming into tune, your actions becoming an extension of your authentic essence.

These are just a few whispers, and your own clues to transformation may manifest in unique ways. The key is staying present and mindful of the subtle shifts within and around you. Keep a journal, practice meditation, or simply take moments of quiet reflection to listen to the whispers of your BIG self.

Celebrate each change, each ripple of growth, as they are the beautiful melody of your ongoing evolution. Embrace the journey, trust the process, and know that you are becoming the masterpiece of your own "BIGNESS" with every step you take.

As you practice gratitude and daily affirmations, something starts changing inside. Old ways of thinking fade away, making space for a new lifestyle. The pull of fitting into society's norms becomes weaker because you're thinking for yourself now, breaking free from the box.

There's a fire burning within, driving you to follow your God-given path. As you become more accustomed to seeking and finding peace and joy within yourself, often through routine body scans or moments of mindfulness, you'll discover a newfound sense of contentment in just being present. It's about finding tranquility in your daily life, knowing that you're evolving into a more authentic and fulfilled version of yourself.

As you begin this journey, you might notice a shift in the people around you. You might find yourself drawn to like-minded individuals who share your desire for growth, while some old connections might start fading. It's not that you're leaving people behind but growing in different directions.

New dreams and bigger visions start taking shape in your mind. You're no longer held captive by the need to be perfect; it's becoming a thing of the past. Instead, you've embraced the idea of doing your best each day, striving for excellence without the weight of perfectionism. There's a newfound satisfaction in knowing that your best effort, consistently given, is more than enough.

Embracing your Bigness isn't just a solitary act of self-growth; it's a cosmic ripple that sends waves through your relationships and inner world. It's like stepping into a new constellation, where your newfound energy magnetizes like-minded souls who resonate with your newfound fire. Conversations become effortless, sparked by shared values and a common thirst for growth. These connections become your guiding stars, offering support, inspiration, and a sense of belonging on this ever-evolving journey.

But sometimes, as your orbit shifts, so do the constellations around you. Gentle departures may occur, not from casting shadows but from simply acknowledging that paths can diverge. Outgrowing connections doesn't signify failure; it's a testament to your evolving landscape, making space for new constellations to align with your Big self.

Once confined by limiting beliefs, your mind expands into a visionary horizon. Dreams that were once whispers become vibrant canvases bursting with possibility. You dare to chase bigger goals, embrace the unknown, and let go of the societal compass that pointed you toward conformity. These visions become your North Star, guiding you towards your own unique Big destination.

But amidst the pursuit of grand visions, perfectionism loosens its grip. You realize that excellence isn't about chasing an unattainable ideal; it's about giving your best, including flaws and vulnerabilities, and finding satisfaction in the journey. This newfound freedom allows you to take risks, explore, and embrace the beauty of imperfection.

The celebration of progress becomes a mantra. Each hurdle overcome, each small step forward, is a cause for quiet joy. You learn to appreciate the consistent effort and the unwavering commitment that fuels your Big climb. This shift transforms the journey itself into a source of fulfillment, where every sunrise is a victory dance.

And slowly, a quiet confidence whispers within you. You begin to understand that your best, offered with honesty and integrity, is more than enough. This self-acceptance becomes your guiding light, freeing you from the need for external validation and allowing you to blossom with genuine authenticity.

- You should choose to embrace your Bigness, for it's not just a personal transformation; it's a beautiful dance with the world around you, a symphony of shifting constellations, soaring dreams, and a heart that whispers, "This is enough."

When life throws curveballs and things don't unfold as planned, you've learned to look for the silver lining and trust in a universal flow. There's a belief that even when circumstances seem tough, they're ultimately working out for your good.

Being BIG isn't just about you; it extends to the people who are connected to you in some way. Think about it—on this planet of about 7.8 billion people, there's a vast array of individuals from diverse backgrounds and experiences. Not everyone can relate to or connect with everyone else, and that's okay. But among these billions, a significant number can relate to you and resonate with your experiences and values. These are the folks who are looking for someone like you to build connections and community with. It's about finding and fostering those meaningful connections among the sea of humanity.

When you're stuck in shrink or copy mode—trying to fit into molds that aren't yours—you might miss out on connecting with those individuals who are meant to be part of your journey. It's like two ships passing in the night; both you and those meant for you might be adrift, unable to find each other. This can lead to settling for a community that doesn't quite align with who you are.

In this scenario, you might feel a sense of disconnection—like you don't truly belong or aren't fully welcomed. There's this yearning for something more, a longing for a community that truly resonates with your values and experiences. It's about recognizing that being true to yourself is crucial in attracting and nurturing connections with those who genuinely understand and support you.

Picture it as two ships sailing through the night, destined for connection but veering past each other, unseen and unnoticed. You and the individuals who could deeply resonate with your essence might be sailing parallel but missing the chance to intersect. It's a missed opportunity, leaving both parties adrift in a sea of missed connections.

This can lead to settling for communities or relationships that don't entirely align with who you are at your core. It's like trying to fit puzzle pieces from different sets—they might superficially seem to match, but they don't truly belong together. This mismatch can result in a sense of dissonance, where you feel out of place or not entirely understood. By shedding the borrowed identities and allowing yourself to shine authentically, you open the channels for genuine connections. When you embrace your true self, you emit a beacon that attracts those who align with your values, interests, and beliefs. These are the individuals who can complement your journey, understand your aspirations, and support your growth.

Authenticity is the magnet that draws your tribe closer, fostering connections that resonate on a deeper level. It's about finding your community—the one that celebrates your uniqueness, respects your individuality, and encourages you to flourish as your true self. And in doing so, you create a space where you don't have to shrink or copy; you can expand, evolve, and thrive in the company of those who truly see and appreciate you for who you are.

Your "BIGNESS" isn't just about personal growth—it's intertwined with your God-given purpose, contributing to a sense of accomplishment and fulfillment. As you embrace Being BIG, I hope you've started envisioning a brighter world, driven by your decision to show up authentically.

The concept of embracing your "BIG" transcends mere personal growth; it intertwines with a deeper, innate purpose, a calling that feels like God's gift. It's about recognizing that your unique qualities, experiences, and aspirations are intricately woven into the fabric of a greater purpose, contributing to your fulfillment and the betterment of the world around you.

When you decide to "Be BIG," you align with your God-given purpose—an inherent calling that beckons you to contribute, create, and impact the world around you. This isn't just about achieving personal milestones; it's about recognizing your role in the grander scheme of things. Your authenticity, your genuine self, is a crucial piece of the larger puzzle that shapes a brighter, more vibrant world.

As you embrace walking in your BIG, envisioning a brighter world becomes more than a distant dream—it becomes a palpable reality. Your decision to show up authentically, to be true to who you are, becomes a catalyst for positive change. It's the ripple effect of authenticity, sparking inspiration in others to do the same and creating a collective energy that propels progress and transformation.

This journey isn't solitary; it's a communal experience. As you embrace your authentic self, you become a beacon, inviting others to join in creating a world fueled by authenticity, compassion, and purpose. Your decision to show up authentically becomes a catalyst for change, inspiring others to embrace their BIG and contribute their unique gifts to the world.

So, embracing your BIGNESS isn't just a personal quest; it's a collective endeavor to weave a tapestry of purpose and fulfillment. It's about fostering a world where authenticity reigns supreme, each individual feels empowered to contribute meaningfully, and the ripple effects of genuine self-expression create a more vibrant, interconnected, and harmonious world for all. I see a future where everyone sheds the skin of mediocrity and bursts forth in their full, vibrant spectrum of potential. It's not a solo act; it's a symphony, each soul playing its unique melody in harmony with the grand orchestra of humanity.

Imagine a ripple effect emanating from every act of authenticity, every brushstroke of purpose. A barista pouring a latte with mindfulness, a teacher igniting curiosity in their students, a carpenter crafting furniture with love – each action, however small, sends ripples outward, shimmering with the potential for positive change. This Being BIG isn't a hashtag or a trend; it's a revolution of the spirit. It's about rediscovering the inherent nobility in every human being, the spark of divinity that ignites compassion, creativity, and a fierce determination to make the world a better place. It's about shaking off the shackles of fear and stepping into the light, not just for ourselves but for the sake of every creature, every blade of grass, and every drop of water in this fragile, magnificent ecosystem we call Earth.

I envision a world where our collective authenticity becomes an infectious force, a wave of purpose washing away negativity and indifference. We'll see artists painting murals that heal hearts, entrepreneurs building businesses that uplift communities, and scientists unlocking secrets that benefit all living things. This isn't some utopian fantasy; it's the logical extension of the ripple effect, the inevitable outcome of a world where everyone chooses to be their best version. And I, for one, am ready to be a part of it. I'll start with my actions and choices, striving to be the BIGGEST version of myself, the standard of authenticity in a world that desperately needs it. And as I do, I'll hold onto the hope that my ripples, however small, will merge with others, creating a tidal wave of positive change that washes away the darkness and illuminates the path toward a brighter future for all.

So, let's join hands, hearts, souls, and voices. Let's paint the world BIG, one beautiful and colorful individual at a time. Together, the Be BIG Collective is a choir. Everyone has their unique voice, whether you're a soprano, alto, tenor, or bass, all coming together to let out a harmonious and unified sound. The sound of BIG! It's time to step onto the stage and sing the songs of our authentic selves with a melody that will resonate through the ages, a testament to the power of Being BIG together. Let's do this!

Made in the USA
Middletown, DE
21 February 2024